Compact Cymru

Snowdonia Scrambles

Mike Peacock

Gwasg Carreg Gwalch

First published in 2020

ISBN: 978-1-84524-293-0
Cover design: Eleri Owen

Published by Gwasg Carreg Gwalch,
12 Iard yr Orsaf, Llanrwst, Wales LL26 0EH
tel: 01492 642031
email: books@carreg-gwalch.cymru
website: www.carreg-gwalch.cymru

Acknowledgements

I would like to thank all those people who accompanied me during my investigations, particularly as often my companions would probably have preferred to have been on a sunny ridge rather than in some dank gorge: Mark Cooper, Pete Early, Chris Earing, Hannah Coustick, Jen Farrelly, Will Farrelly, Stuart Gillies, Gareth Harvey, Rachel Harvey, Tom Hecht, Dave Jackson, Adrian Luescher, Fred Maier, Jon McMullin, Tom Mills, Michèle Oakley, Si Oakley, Chris Peacock, Adam Pearce, Owain Rice, Geth Roberts, Kirsty Roberts, John Stringer, and my wife Susan. Additional thanks are due to Gareth, Hannah, Owain, Rachel and Tom H for proof reading the draft. I am grateful to Adam Pearce for providing help with some of the Welsh translations. Thanks are also due to John Appleby who pointed me in the direction of some gorges I might otherwise have missed, and for hosting an article about my exploits on his Footless Crow website. I am grateful to Sam Bosanquet and Joe Roberts at NRW who gave environmental guidance. Sam wrote the section on gorge ecology and provided other snippets of bryophyte-related text that have been inserted elsewhere into the book. He also contributed several photos. Finally, thanks to Tony Ryan at the BMC for granting permission to include the BMC's participation statement.

Finally, I dedicate this book to the Bangor UMWC who introduced me to the wonderful hills and mountains of Snowdonia. Long may they continue to do the same for other students at Bangor University.

BMC Participation Statement

Climbing, hill walking and mountaineering are activities with a danger of personal injury or death. Participants in these activities should be aware of and accept these risks and be responsible for their own actions and involvement.

Contents

Introduction

Scrambling in North Wales

North Wales is blessed with a wealth of excellent scrambling. This was highlighted with Steve Ashton's classic book "Scrambles in Snowdonia", first published in 1980. This book focused on a relatively small geographical area, and covered the Glyderau, Carneddau, Yr Wyddfa (Snowdon) and Eifionydd. In 2005 "Scrambles and Easy Climbs in Snowdonia" was published, which covered a much wider geographical area. The book contained a handful of new scrambles, including ones on Cadair Idris and Rhinog Fawr, but the book was perhaps aimed more at climbers as it focused mainly on long low-grade climbs rather than scrambles. Another handful of 'new' scrambles appeared in the Climbers' Club Ogwen guidebook in 2010; many of these were old, low grade climbs that had been reassessed as scrambles, but some were described on cliffs such as Tryfan's West Face and Carnedd y Filiast; locations usually spurned by scramblers. Most recently, Garry Smith's "North Wales Scrambles" was released in 2014. This treads much the same geographical ground as "Scrambles in Snowdonia" but throws in a few new routes, and features numerous excellent photographs.

So why another scrambling guide for Wales? The first reason is that the gorges and streams have been unfairly ignored. In the Lake District gill (gorge) scrambling is relatively popular, and the routes have been described and published. The same is not true of Wales. Although commercial companies operate in a few gorges, most are neglected. I am sure that some locals and visitors have explored some of these routes, but during my explorations I only ever encountered one group that was not a commercial venture.

The second reason is that the majority of previously described mountain scrambles have been restricted to the most popular areas in the north of the national park. However, there is plenty of rock elsewhere, on large and small hills. This book therefore aims to offer new scrambles, in gorges and streams, on crags and ridges. Not all of the routes are of a three star quality, although many are. In many ways, I would draw a comparison between this book and the two "Scrambles in the Lake District" volumes, which featured gorges and gills, as well as highlighting short scrambles on lesser hills and outcrops.

I hope this book goes beyond a mere scrambling guidebook; I hope it entices people away from the honeypots to new areas and new adventures; it is a calling for people to discover more of Wales and to get off the beaten track.

What is Scrambling?

Scrambling is the middle ground between hillwalking and climbing. It involves the use of hands and feet to ascend rocky, pathless ground. The difficulty covers a wide range, and some high-end scrambles are also recognised as low-grade rock climbs.

The Scrambles

The scrambles in this book vary considerably. Those based around watercourses can be divided into two broad categories; streams and gorges. Generally, stream scrambles will be in a mountain setting, and the environment will be open. Contrary to this, gorges are more likely to be at a lower altitude, escape might be difficult, and trees may shade the gorge. For the rocky scrambles, many are found on the high mountains, but some are also on lesser hills. They mostly share one commonality; they go somewhere. They may lead you to a summit or a viewpoint, or they may be one part of a link up leading to a high mountain top. In this respect, I hope I am following Steve Ashton's philosophical definition of scrambling; that scrambling should follow a scenic, defined line, rather than seeking out rock for the sake of it. Some of the routes are suitable for a summer evening after work, and some are better enjoyed as part of a long mountain day.

The scrambles are divided by geographical area, although this is somewhat subjective, as some routes can be approached from multiple starting points (and therefore different areas). Each chapter begins with a description of the geographical area, and ends with some speculative notes as to where more scrambles may be hiding. Each individual route has a short introduction which describes the character or quality of that scramble, as well as any particularly sensitive ecological issues. There then follows a rough translation of the route name (if it is Welsh), a summary of the scramble, details of how to approach the scramble, a route description, then details on how to get back down, or suggested options to continue the day.

Gradings

I have kept to the Welsh tradition of using grades 1, 2 and 3, with borderline routes indicated as 1/2 or 2/3.

Grade 1 routes should be relatively straightforward. Difficulties should be minor, and escape should be easy. These routes should be a good step up for experienced hill walkers who are looking to start scrambling.

Grade 2 routes are more serious. The technical difficulty of the scrambling will be higher, and escape may be difficult or even impossible. Route finding may be tricky

Grade 3 routes are the hardest. Only experienced scramblers should attempt these routes. They may involve exposed and/or technical scrambling, or passages of committing deep water without escape. Grading is subjective however, and this book has been written over many years. The difficulty of a scramble can change depending on weather, time of year, water levels, or even a scrambler's frame of mind. Do not be surprised if you disagree with some of my gradings. It is worth noting that gorge scrambling and mountain scrambling are inherently different games, requiring different skill sets. A grade 3 in the mountains may be exposed and airy, whilst a grade 3 in a gorge may not be exposed but might feature technical traverses or committing sections of deep water. The two routes, though graded the same, may not be comparable. Read the route descriptions to get a feel for the difficulties of any particular route.

Star Ratings

Again, I have kept to tradition by using star ratings to highlight the quality of individual scrambles, with *** being the highest rating. However, do not let this deter you from visiting low or no-starred scrambles. They may still lead you to a memorable day out in a new place.

Sensitive Vegetation

Care should be taken not to disturb vegetation for all the described scrambles. However, particularly sensitive ones are marked with a (V).

Equipment and Safety

For all routes it is assumed that the reader has a suitable map and the knowledge of how to read it. Although maps are provided showing the locations of the scrambles, these are only given for context and should not be used to navigate with. For those routes in mountain environments mountain skills are needed; the ability to use compass and to navigate; to pace distances and evaluate terrain and weather; to administer first aid. Such advice is beyond the scope of this book, but numerous books concerning mountain skills exist. The Mountain Training books are a good place to start: http://www.mountain-training.org/publications/hill-walking.

All of the gorges in this book have been done without buoyancy aids or wetsuits. That is, they have been approached in a scrambling fashion, rather than a canyoning fashion. The scrambling approach calls for techniques such as traversing gorge walls, whereas a canyoner would simply swim across a pool. The scrambler always aims to stay relatively dry, although wading is often called for. Where a route features particularly deep water this is noted in the text, and the reader may prefer to resort to the safety of a buoyancy aid.

Generally for gorge scrambling, usual mountain clothing is sufficient. There are a few notable exceptions to standard mountain kit. Firstly, for any scrambles where wading might be necessary lightweight, quick-drying shorts or trousers are ideal. Trousers that zip off into shorts can be even better. Either way, trousers or shorts should offer lots of freedom of leg movement. It almost need not be said that jeans are out of the question, which get extremely heavy when wet. This is important especially if the chosen route is in a mountain environment, or where a continuation onto the mountain is planned after the scramble. Wet trousers in cold weather and strong winds can leads to hypothermia if a person is improperly equipped.

A second consideration is the choice of footwear. Walking boots are wise if a route is in a mountain environment, but if a scramble is roadside than trainers or approach shoes may be preferred due to their lightness. The third option is that of specialist canyoning boots such as the 5.10 Canyoneer. A useful tip for particularly slimy routes is to carry a pair of thick woollen socks which can be placed over the outside of the boots to provide extra grip. Dry bags are also useful for keeping kit (and car keys!) dry within a rucksack, if the worst should happen and a fall or slip results in a dunking.

The question of whether to take a rope when scrambling is much debated. Whilst it is often emphasised that unroped, exposed scrambling is the most dangerous form of mountaineering, many argue that a large part of the appeal comes from moving light and unencumbered over interesting terrain. Certainly, carrying a rope is prudent for the harder and more committing scrambles, but it also must be stressed that the proper knowledge of how to use such equipment must also be carried. It may occasionally be the case that retreat is necessary, and abseil techniques may be necessary for this to be successful, as many gorges have steep and uncompromising side walls that limit lateral escape. Extra care should be taken in the big gorges; ropes and deep water are not a good mix.

There are many scrambles within this book where escape is often simple, and for these a lightweight approach may be opted for. For those without the knowledge of how to use ropes, several long slings and karabiners can be helpful bits of kit. These can be used for a variety of purposes; to provide extra handholds on a blank section of rock, or to pull up rucksacks to allow a particularly tricky section to be climbed without the burden of a bag.

The use of a helmet is another issue that is often debated amongst scramblers. For the pursuit of gorge scrambling it is highly recommended that a helmet be worn. Loose rock is common, and in the more impressive ravines it is possible for debris to fall (or even be thrown) down the side walls. Slimy rock can also lead to a scrambler slipping over, and a helmet will add some protection in such situations.

Gorge scrambling is uniquely different compared to traditional mountain scrambling. Wet rock and slime are frequently encountered. These can be unnerving for beginners, but over time the seasoned gorge scrambler learns to read the terrain ahead; to evaluate rock quality, and how slippery a rock may be. For those new to the game it is best to start on grade 1 routes that have easy escape options, and to proceed slowly. Nevertheless, all scrambling is dangerous, both in gorges and in the hills. Loose rock, treacherous vegetation, changes in the weather, and other unforeseen hazards have to be dealt with.

Finally, it is impossible to discuss safety requirements without mentioning water levels. Wales is a land of rain. After heavy rain the mountain streams turn to foaming torrents, limiting any chance of a scramble, whilst the big lowland gorges become flooded with roaring torrents. Water levels can rise alarmingly quickly. However, it is possible to find sport in such conditions. One option is to pick a route with a small catchment, thus limiting the amount of water in the stream. For instance, when the mountain streams have been in spate I have sometimes found some of the Gwydyr Forest gorges to be relatively dry. A second option is to carefully select a shallow, low grade route; some of the easy routes can be entertaining, provided that the party have resigned themselves to a soaking. One useful tool is NRW's website showing river levels found at https://naturalresources.wales/evidence-and-data/maps/check-river-levels/. It must be remembered that any final decision on water levels can only be made upon arriving on the stream bank, and a final call on safety resides solely with the scrambler. Even apparently innocuous-looking watercourses can be powerful and can knock a scrambler off their feet. If in doubt, turn away and go for a walk in the rain; the scrambles will remain for another day.

If an accident does occur, then call mountain rescue; dial 999, ask for the police, then ask for mountain rescue. Ideally, supply mountain rescue with a grid reference, the nature of the accident, details of the casualty, the number of people in the group, how well equipped the party is, and contact numbers. If signal is poor, it is now possible to text the emergency services. You can register for this system at http://www.emergencysms.org.uk/.

Access

Access information is given for each route. However, access land and rights of way can change. It is the responsibility of the scrambler to ensure that their progress across the land is legal.

Finally

Bear in mind that this book can only take you so far. I have described the routes as best I can, but times may well arise when you struggle to match my descriptions with the terrain in front of you. I have certainly found this on occasions when using other scrambling guides. Needless to say a scrambler must have skills that are learned through experience. It is up to you to employ these skills and to decide if it is safe to continue, or whether a retreat or escape is prudent. You must bear in mind that hillwalking and scrambling both come with inherent risks; there is a real danger of injury or death, as reflected in the BMC's Participation Statement. Ensure that you have the knowledge, skills, ability and equipment to minimise these risks.

The Ecology of Gorges and Responsible Use

By Sam Bosanquet, Natural Resources Wales

Wales' rocky ravines provide ideal conditions for a wide range of mosses and liverworts to grow. Some of these tiny plants are restricted in Wales to a handful of ravines in Eryri and Meirionnydd; others are more widespread. The rarest, some of which are found in colonies no bigger than a post card, are sensitive to frost and drought and tend to be extremely small: only a few millimetres long. Constant water flow, steep rocky banks and an overhanging tree canopy provide perfect conditions for them. Seeing them requires a close search of the vertical sides of boulders or rock faces, especially where cascades make the air constantly moist.

Larger, commoner mosses have evolved to cope with the pounding of water, and grow in or alongside streams. These moss patches are often home to aquatic insects, which in turn feed fish and dippers. Rock faces set back from a stream may support luxuriant carpets or cushions of moss. The bouldery woodlands, which are particularly characteristic of north-west Wales, are often also covered with large leafy liverworts that thrive on the shady environment and damp air. Although these species have evolved to survive the occasional big spates that roll through the ravines, sustained erosion by feet and hands can cause irreversible damage to their communities.

Please help keep these temperate rainforests lush and vibrant:

1. Avoid rubbing against or climbing on vegetated rock faces, you may accidentally brush off something really rare.
2. Stick to established paths or sheep tracks when away from the immediate streamside to help prevent accidental damage to the mossy woodland.
3. Remember: "If it's green keep it pristine!"

A fragile Wilson's filmy-fern growing out of a cushion of the red-coloured liverwort Mylia taylorii. Photo by Sam Bosanquet

These guidelines apply for all of the gorges in the book. However, routes that have more sensitive or important species are marked with a (V).

The rare ravine moss Campylopus setifolius forms loose cushions and can easily be knocked off by a careless boot placement.
Photo by Sam Bosanquet

Dyffryn Ogwen (Ogwen Valley)

Undoubtedly, Dyffryn Ogwen is one of the finest outdoor playgrounds in all of Wales. People come here to walk the wide grassy ridges of the Carneddau, to scramble over rocky Tryfan and the Glyderau, to climb on the Idwal Slabs and other fine crags, or just to admire the mountains from the car parks.

With such a wealth of rock to play on, the gorges and streams of the valley have thus been neglected, but they offer some fine sport for those seeking something different rather than tackling Tryfan's North Ridge for the umpteenth time. A day on Creigiau Gleision at the far end of the valley is another ignored gem that offers solitude with some added scrambling. Many of the scrambles here can be sampled on a warm summer evening, or can be done early in the day as a prelude to moving on to higher ground.

For the purposes of this section, Dyffryn Ogwen is used to encompass the area from Bethesda to Idwal Cottage (properly Nant Ffrancon), and onwards to Capel Curig (Nant y Benglog). The routes described fall on the slopes of both the Glyderau and Carneddau.

There are many possible bases to launch explorations from; there are campsites and bunkhouses in the valley at Gwern Gof Isaf and Gwern Gof Uchaf, as well as the Dolgam and Bryn Tyrch campsites at Capel Curig. Both Idwal Cottage and Capel Curig have youth hostels, and there are numerous hotels and bed and breakfasts scattered elsewhere such as Bethesda and Betws-y-Coed.

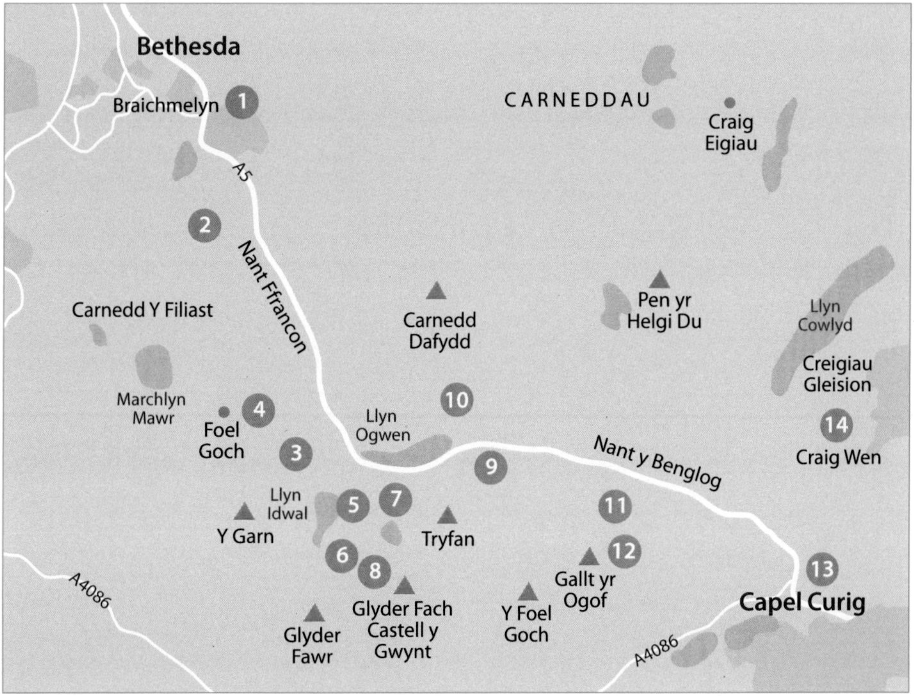
Bethesda
Braichmelyn
1
CARNEDDAU
Craig
Eigiau
A5
2
Nant Ffrancon
Carnedd Y Filiast
Carnedd
Dafydd
Pen yr
Helgi Du
Llyn
Cowlyd
Creigiau
Gleision
Marchlyn
Mawr
4
Foel
Goch
10
Llyn
Ogwen
14
3
9
Nant y Benglog
Craig Wen
Llyn
Idwal
5
7
11
Y Garn
Tryfan
6
12
8
Gallt yr
Ogof
13
A4086
Capel Curig
Glyder Fach
Castell y
Gwynt
Y Foel
Goch
Glyder
Fawr
A4086

1. Afon Caseg & Afon Llafar (1 or 3*) (V)

This has to rate as one of the strangest routes in this book, simply because it starts just off the streets of Bethesda. Although not much height is gained it makes a decent start to a day on the Carneddau. The (optional) hard crux is a particularly satisfying sequence of moves at the end of the route, but the middle section is mainly walking. As the rivers drain huge catchments, a dry spell may be needed for a trip to be feasible. There are some sensitive bryophytes but mostly these are on the sides of rocks alongside cascades. Although several rights of way intersect with the river, it is not on access land.

Meaning: The river of the mare, the noisy river.

Summary: River scrambling up a wooded gorge with a pleasing walking section sandwiched between a good but short start and finish.

Conditions: The rock is generally sound apart from on the crux at the end. Moss features but this is unproblematic.

Height Gain: 55m

Approach: There is parking in Bethesda. Walk south out of the centre of Bethesda along the main road (A5). At SH 626659 take another road left (eastish) and follow this. Just before the bridge over the Afon Caseg turn right (south-east) along a minor road. This ends and a right of way leads off left in front of a house towards the river at SH 631661.

Ascent: Gaining the river bank here is troublesome, which is good as the first fall in a short gorge cannot be climbed. Enter onto the river above this; the gradient is relaxed and the channel wide. The river forks but keep to the right branch, hopping rocks then scrambling up a smooth slab on its left side. Weave under branches then climb a boulder via a runnel carrying water on its right. Ahead is a low-relief rib in the middle of the channel. This can be gained by the left bank (ducking under trees) then stepping across. Above this the

stream relaxes and flows through scenic woodland.

The best bet is to stick to the left bank, with various short bouldery traverses presenting themselves. These can all be avoided by walking along the bank. Continue up, passing under a pipe. Just after passing the football pitch on the left the river splits again. The left fork is the

1. The short central rib; 2 The hard final traverse on the Afon Llafar.

continuation of the Afon Caseg, but stick to the right onto the Afon Llafar. Walk up beside the river until things get interesting again. The next obstacle is an entertaining (and slightly vegetated) traverse on the right; although mossy, this offers good footing. Both banks offer more optional traverses until the finale arrives.

The sides of the river rise up and (at the time of writing) a metal sink sits in the water. The watercourse turns left above a scenic cascade, backed by a crumbling cliff. Traverse in on the right (past a car door! – perhaps long gone now?) then climb the short central rib between the two waterfalls. Beyond another mossy section the crux waits. To keep at grade 1 take this last pool on the right. For those who want a challenge the left wall can be traversed at grade 3. The rock is less sound than that lower down, but a fall will just deposit the unlucky scrambler in the water. Move along the wall with good ledges for feet. After a few metres a step across is made and the corner reached. At the corner the key is a hold hidden behind the back of a block which facilitates an arrival to safe ground.

Above is a bridge carrying the minor dead-end road from Gerlan. Climb a fence to gain the road.

Usual Descents: The road can be followed back into Bethesda.

Combinations: From the track to the nearby water works a well-used path leads into Cwm Llafar. Scramblers can take this to the end of the cwm and enjoy the classic grade 1 of Crib Lem Spur. A walking option is to proceed over Mynydd Du and follow the faint path up to Carnedd Dafydd, perhaps as a precursor to a round of Cwm Llafar. Those of a desperate nature could scramble up the Afon Wen (SH 675663) on Foel Grach, but most of that route involves avoiding small mossy waterfalls with little real scrambling. Another worthwhile target is the North-East Ridge of Yr Elen, which provides an enjoyable way up, but with no proper scrambling.

2. Fronllwyd Slabs (1 or 2 or 3)

Fronllwyd is the spur that runs north from the summit of Carnedd y Filiast. Perhaps once it offered a graceful, curving descent down to Bethesda, but now it has been obscenely curtailed by the workings of Penrhyn Quarry, often claimed as the largest slate quarry in the world. Nevertheless, a peaty path runs through the heather along the crest of Fronllwyd, and it offers a delightful walk up Carnedd y Filiast (provided the eyes are not directed back at that monstrous chasm). The described scramble provides a way of gaining this path. It is contrived, but enjoyable.

Meaning: Grey breast.

Summary: Pick-your-own-difficulty scrambling up a series of non-serious slabs, where escape is always possible.

Conditions: The grip of the rock is excellent. There are occasional blocks that look loose; treat them with care.

Height Gain: 130m

Approach: An approach can be made from Bethesda/Ogwen Bank by taking the path (and cycle track) through Penrhyn Quarry. Once through the quarry the path enters a long straight and a series of broken slabs are visible running right back up the hillside. Leave the path via a gate on the right and walk across boggy ground, aiming for a lone hawthorn tree by the lowest slab (approx. SH 626640). Alternatively, there is space for a few cars on the single-track road at SH 631633 (be careful to not block passing places). From here walk back north along the road and keep straight onto the cycle path when the road turns right.

Ascent: There is no point in describing an exact line; seek out difficulty and variations at will. The first small slab is broken and vegetated but things improve after this. The route consists of tiers of slabs separated by easy ground. Easy lines can be made by using the cracks, whilst

harder routes can be contrived up the blank slabs. If a tier appears too difficult, a walk left or right below it should bring an easier option.

Notable features further up include a few metres of dry stone wall, and a bouldery canyon running across the route. Continue up, seeking out the best rock until it peters out. Now comes the painful part; a path lies not far ahead but reaching it involves flailing through heather of an extraordinary depth. This will be the source of much cursing on a hot, sunny morning as tempers fray with the exertion.

Usual Descents: If it can be found, a small path can be followed back down into Cwm Ceunant.

Combinations: Carnedd y Filiast can be reached by following the path along the crest. From here Mynydd Perfedd, Elidir Fawr and Foel Goch are all worthy targets. One viable descent back to Bethesda can be made by crossing a style below Mynydd Perfedd where a little-used path descends on a spur between Cwm Perfedd and Cwm Bual. It runs out almost immediately but a pleasant tramp leads down to the field boundary where the stream can be crossed. From here slant down to reach the road somewhere north of Maes Caradoc.

A view of the Fronllwyd Slabs

3. Cwm Cywion Stream (1 or 2 or 3*)

This route takes the stream that flows down from the remote Llyn Cywion that sits below Foel Goch and Y Garn. The stream is unnamed on maps. Although it begins only ten minutes from Idwal Cottage it provides solitude and a new view of Dyffryn Ogwen. It is a route of two stages; the lower watercourse is open in nature whilst the upper gorge closes in to form a short ravine.

Meaning: Cwm of the chicks.

Summary: Escapable scrambling up an open streambed, followed by a short walk in a ravine. The final section consists of more short falls.

Conditions: The stream is a bit slimy in places, and there is some loose rock, though neither detracts from the enjoyment of the trip.

Height Gain: 200m

Approach: From the car park at Idwal Cottage take the minor road past the youth hostel and beyond Yr Hafod. You soon reach a bridge over a stream flowing down a steep gorge from the mountainside (SH 642607). This is the start of the route.

Ascent: Walk up to the first fall. This doesn't give a gentle introduction to the route; despite the left side looking tempting a central route is best. Climb up from the right end of the central boulder in the stream on slippery rock, with holds improving with height (grade 2). Above this, scramble up the central dry rib. If you are deterred by this first fall, leave the bed and ascend a grassy runnel on the left. Regain the bed above this. Climb a few little cascades and pass a bridge. From here the view opens out and the route ahead can be appraised; small falls can be seen in front of the majestic backdrop of Y Garn and Pinnacle Crag.

Continue up the stream bed over small obstacles (including one waterfall topped by a large dead tree), and step over an old wire fence that crosses the watercourse. Surmount a greasy fall and the stream opens out again. Here, make the most of

1. *Chris Peacock on the hard start of the Cwm Cywion stream; 2 Wetter is better?*

dry scrambling on its left bank before arriving at the base of a wide waterfall. In spate conditions this is best avoided by walking around, but when water levels are low a wet ascent can be made up the left hand side, though be careful with suspect rock.

Beyond this continue up the stream, passing the remains of an old wooden bridge in the channel. Further up the stream makes a right turn and enters a runnel. Before tackling this obstacle, an entertaining traverse of a few metres can be had on the slabby left-hand wall. Continue on up to reach a longer waterslide (easy grade 2), which is best ascended on its right hand side and is much easier after a dry spell. Above this you soon reach a larger, more intimidating fall; this is the second (grade 3) crux. Most will be happy to walk up to examine this large fall then leave the stream and walk around to enter the upper gorge (note a wall traversing the slopes at this point). The more adventurous will make a hard

ascent using holds on the far left, though the consequences of a slip from the top onto the rocks below would be severe.

Above, the stream flows along a gentle gradient in a ravine. Either walk up, or traverse along the right-hand wall at the level of the water. This section ends at a small pool, beyond which more small falls can be climbed leading into remote Cwm Cywion.

Usual Descents: A direct descent can be made beside the stream to return to the road. An alternative is to pick up a path beside the previously mentioned wall. This can be followed south-east into Cwm Idwal where a path leads to Idwal Cottage.

Combinations: One option is to take an unmarked path that winds up Foel Goch via the Y Llymllwyd spur. For a more adventurous day, pick up a faint but well-used traversing path that crosses a scree slope before depositing you at a sheep fold below the vegetated crag of Creigiau Gleision. There are several scrambles here such as The Mushroom Garden (grade 2 – route 4) and Needle's Eye Arête (grade 3). Easy Gully (approximately SH 631610) is the wide scree shoot at the back left (south) of the cwm, and can be used for upwards progress, but it is steep and loose and not much fun. If a walking day is preferred the traversing path continues across Cwm Coch before entering lonely Cwm Bual (Esgair Gully is another option here – see Further Scrambling Opportunities). The ridge between Foel Goch and Mynydd Perfedd can then be gained using the spur between Cwm Bual and Cwm Perfedd. Another option is to climb Y Garn by an unfrequented route; a vague spur runs up from Cwm Cywion that we could perhaps call the North Spur. It is seen well by following the Nant Cywion into the cwm to the small lake and runs from SH 633603. At its base is the Pinnacle Crag of Cwm Cywion (SH 634603 – note this is a different location to where the OS maps Pinnacle Crag). The spur consists of steep grass and scree, and steepens further towards the top, where the use of hands might be needed to steady oneself. The spur leads out on to the main walking route up to Y Garn around SH 633600.

Llyn Ogwen and Tryfan from the Cwm Cywion stream

4. The Mushroom Garden (2*)

This scramble was previously described in "Scrambles and Easy Climbs in Snowdonia" and is also in the Ogwen Climbers' Club guide under the name South Arête. It lies on Creigiau Gleision on Foel Goch (not to be confused with the Creigiau Gleision above Llyn Crafnant) in the Glyderau. Creigiau Gleision is a sprawling mass of gullies and towers and pinnacles, and much of the rock is vegetated. This route follows a vague line up the left side of the cliff, and offers much scope to explore. The scrambling is mediocre, but the atmosphere and outlook more than compensate, and the crag is usually quiet.

Meaning: N/A

Summary: Exploratory scrambling up a remote crag.

Conditions: The route starts up a rubbly gully and much of the scrambling is vegetated. Best left for a dry spell.

Height Gain: 150m

Approach: Approach can be made by scrambling the previous route (Nant Cywion) or simply by walking beside the Nant Cywion. From Idwal Cottage take the minor road past the youth hostel and beyond Yr Hafod, until you reach a bridge over a stream flowing down a steep gorge (SH 642607). This is the Nant Cywion. Follow it upwards until a wall comes down to a deep section of the gorge at SH 637604. From here follow a narrow trod that traverses northwards across the scree slopes and leads to Cwm Coch and sheep pens at SH 636610. Continue traversing along the trod into the cwm until reaching a rubbly gully that burrows into the crag at SH 635611. This is Eastern Gully and the start of the route.

Ascent: Proceed up the gully which is loose and scrabbling rather than scrambling, until blocked by a steep wall. Moving right here will lead to the start of Needle's Eye Arête (grade 3), so instead move left out of the gully into open ground. Move upwards, seeking or avoiding difficulties as they present themselves. A larger step is overcome using a ramp that slants leftwards. The scrambling is disappointing, but the rock scenery is excellent, and the views down into the valley more than compensate. Move past a rock tower and into a grass gully with scrambling opportunities on the right side. At one point a small fragment of stone wall has been constructed below a crag (presumably to stop sheep wandering over the cliffs?). Soon the gradient relents as you arrive on the shoulder of Foel Goch, and the summit is about 700 m walk away to the right.

Usual descents: The Y Llymllwyd spur can be used to return to the gorge section on the Nant Cywion. By turning left from the top of the scramble a faint path leads back down.

Combinations: There are no obvious nearby scrambling combinations. The choice is simply to head north to Mynydd Perfedd or Elidir Fawr, or south to Y Garn.

Adam Pearce and Chris Earing enjoying the exposure on the Mushroom Garden

5. Clogwyn y Tarw (1 or 2 or 3)

For those en route to Cwm Bochlwyd there are two scrambling approaches. The Nant Bochlwyd (route 7) is one for those who don't mind wet boots; this is the drier option. Clogwyn y Tarw bounds the very bottom of the Y Gribin ridge and prevents a direct approach. However, a scramble can be contrived along its crest. When combined with the False Gribin and Y Gribin, it provides the start to several hundred metres of scrambling onto the high Glyderau.

Meaning: Crag of the bull.

Summary: Optional scrambling up several outcrops of rock.

Conditions: The rock quality is good.

Height Gain: 80m

Approach: From Idwal Cottage take the path into Cwm Idwal, and along the east shore of the lake. After the path goes through a gate in a wall turn left. This is where the path to Cwm Cneifion heads up across the slopes. Instead, turn ninety degrees left and walk up beside the wall to where it meets the crag (SH 648595).

Ascent: Scramble up from here (quite steep) on excellent rock. For the first few steep walls, there is a choice of line, some of which are quite difficult. Higher up, link together the numerous little walls and outcrops. All difficulties can be flanked by walking up the rough path on the right until the usual path to Y Gribin is reached.

Usual Descents: The rough path can be followed back down to Llyn Idwal.

Combinations: The logical continuation is to scramble up the False Gribin and Y Gribin (both grade 1 – route 8), or to head into Cwm Cneifion to scramble Nameless Rib – route 6. An alternative is to take the path to Bwlch Tryfan where the Miner's Track can be used to gain the eastern slopes of Glyder Fach.

Kirsty Roberts and Tom Hecht on Clogwyn y Tarw

6. Nameless Rib (2*)

Lonely Cwm Cneifion sits high and empty above Cwm Idwal. It sees its fair share of scramblers heading to the popular hard route of Cneifion Arête, and the occasional walker on their way to Seniors' Ridge. A handful perhaps head further into the cwm to scramble Maybe Tower Rib. There is another (almost) unrecorded attraction though; Nameless Rib. This spiky ridge that parallels Cneifion Arête was given a short mention in early editions of Scrambles in Snowdonia but was later removed, perhaps due to the plethora of other high quality routes in the Glyderau. Nevertheless, this author feels that it is worthy of inclusion.

Summary: Pleasant scrambling up a spiky rib leading to a subsidiary ridge.

Conditions: Due to the route's forgotten status the rib is heathery, but this is unproblematic. There are some loose flakes in place so care should be taken, but the rock itself is intrinsically sound.

Height Gain: 120m

Approach: Start at Idwal Cottage. Take a faint path that leaves the lakeside at Llyn Idwal at SH 646596 (just after a gate). Bear uphill but almost immediately turn right on a fainter path that winds into Cwm Cneifion. Another approach from Cwm Bochlwyd contours around the very foot of the Y Gribin ridge and into Cwm Cneifion (you could scramble the Nant Bochlwyd or Clogwyn y Tarw beforehand if approaching this way). The rib is not apparent from below but is found at roughly SH 648588. The best guide is that it lies just to the left of Cneifion Arête which is an obvious steep ridge on the skyline, on the Y Gribin side of the cwm. Nameless Rib takes the right hand edge of a triangular tower (known as The Pinnacle) of heather and rock. To the right of the rib is an easy angled gully. The left edge of The Pinnacle consists of an obviously steeper rib (Pinnacle Edge, a V Diff climb) beside another gully (Pinnacle Gully).

Ascent: Most will be tempted to start from the right hand tip of the rib next to the gully; don't. It is better to start further down and left and climb straight up to meet the crest, or to bypass the first step by scrambling up the gully on the right and attaining the rib this way. Once established on the crest it is just a case of climbing up. Difficulties can generally be flanked on the left or right. At first escape can often be made to the right, back into the gully, but at some sections this becomes impossible.

The situation itself is fantastic, with a short drop on the right into the gully, and the rib falling away to the left to reveal Llyn Idwal and the Nant Ffrancon. The rock gives excellent grip, but some flakes should be tested for their solidness. Eventually the rib runs out at a level section to meet the gully, but a final pinnacled section of ridge rears up ahead. Climb this, again dodging to the left or right if need be to avoid harder sections. At the top comes the surprise; the rib does not abut against the Y Gribin ridge as might be supposed, but is joined by Pinnacle Edge to form a little summit of its own, with a gully on either side. From here it is a case of scrambling up a short distance on rock and grass to gain the Y Gribin ridge by the 'football pitch'.

Usual descents: Descend down Y Gribin to Llyn Bochlwyd, then take the path beside the Nant Bochlwyd back to Idwal Cottage.

Combinations: Upwards progress is made by climbing Y Gribin (grade 1 – route 8), then a decision must be made to go west to Glyder Fawr (perhaps descend the Devil's Kitchen path, or forge on to Y Garn) or east to Glyder Fach (take the Miner's Track down to Bwlch Tryfan and on to Llyn Bochlwyd).

'Don't look down'. Rachal Harvey on Nameless Rib

7. Nant Bochlwyd (1*) (V)

This short stream scramble rises into Cwm Bochlwyd. Despite a good path running along its bank it is rarely ascended which is a shame; it provides a much more enjoyable alternative to slogging up the path, and can be used as an alternative to reach the False Gribin and Y Gribin. There is quite a range of bryophytes in the stream, but nothing too sensitive to restrict access.

Meaning: Bochlwyd (grey cheek) stream.

Summary: A brief scramble up an open stream, with escape possible at any time.

Conditions: Loose and slimy rock both feature to some extent.

Height Gain: 70m

Approach: From Idwal Cottage take the left-hand path towards Cwm Idwal until another path forks off left across boggy ground. This leads to the Nant Bochlwyd (SH 655597).

Ascent: Enter the channel below a series of steep cascades. Begin on the right side before switching to easy-angled slabs on the left side. Continue up with a choice of possible lines until the gradient eases and Llyn Bochlwyd is reached.

Usual Descents: A path on the west bank leads back to Idwal Cottage.

Combinations: From Cwm Bochlwyd there are numerous scrambling options. You could contour into Cwm Cneifion for Nameless Rib – route 6. Alternately, Bristly Ridge, False Gribin and Y Gribin (all grade 1) provide popular routes onto the Glyderau, and the main face of Glyder Fach hosts a variety of scrambles across the grades.

Si Oakley (1) and the author (2) on the Nant Bochlwyd.

8. The False Gribin, Y Gribin and Castell y Gwynt (1*)

The False Gribin was included in Scrambles in Snowdonia, but never seems to attract many scramblers. This is a shame for, when combined with Clogwyn y Tarw or Nant Bochlwyd, and Y Gribin itself, it is possible to ascend Glyder Fawr or Glyder Fach with minimal walking and maximum scrambling. Y Gribin is a minor classic as Ogwen scrambles go. Or perhaps, it would be if it didn't have to compete with the longer, harder, and more exposed route of Bristly Ridge on the other side of Cwm Bochlwyd. Although the False Gribin and Y Gribin are described elsewhere they are briefly summarised here for ease of reference. Castell y Gwynt offers a final flourish on rock almost to the summit of Glyder Fach.

Once in Cwm Bochlwyd, proceed around the west side of the lake on faint paths to approximately SH 653590. The False Gribin is the broad ridge that leads up to Y Gribin itself. The first section consists of numerous small rocky buttresses, interspersed with boggy ground. Pick any line through these, with a variety of difficulty levels available. The interest level increases further up, as the ridge coalesces into a steep buttress split by ledges and terraces with a choice of line and difficulty, until level ground is reached at the base of the Y Gribin ridge itself (aptly referred to as the 'football pitch'). It is possible to avoid the crest of Y Gribin by following a loose path on the right side of the ridge, although this still involves scrambling. The crest itself presents solid grade 1 scrambling, with a large drop into Cwm Bochlwyd. Obstacles include slabs, arêtes and runnels, with diversions off the crest to the right to avoid anything too intimidating. Eventually the ridge abuts against the grassy plateau between Glyder Fawr and Glyder Fach.

A final micro-scramble can be enjoyed on Castell y Gwynt (castle of the winds, SH 654581), the shattered crown of rock over to the left on the way to Glyder Fach. Many people scramble upwards through the weird architecture of this place in an ad hoc way, but there is a *perfect line*. It is found by following the main path around the base of Castell y Gwynt. Look out for a procession of spiky ribs that run up through the castell to its summit; this is the line. Follow the line of spikes as religiously as possible. Early on is a man-eating chimney that presents an amusing challenge, and beyond the scrambling continues to entertain. The scrambling is on excellent rock, and there is a sense of exposure with mild drops from the ribs. The small summit of the castell is soon reached. Hill-baggers take note: this is the only 3000ft summit that is a Nuttall but not a Hewitt. A short downclimb from the summit leads to level ground, and a final few metres of scrambling brings about the summit of Glyder Fach.

Dave Jackson admiring the views to Tryfan from Y Gribin

9. Tryfan Bach Gully Route (2**)

The great wedge-shaped slab of Tryfan Bach sits beside the A5 in the shadow of its namesake. Most days it is busy due to its proximity to the road and its popularity with new climbers. There are, however, two scrambles on it; a grade 3 route ascends cracks on the left-hand side whilst this easier route follows a gully in the middle of the crag. It provides a good way to begin an assault on the east face of Tryfan.

Meaning: Little Tryfan (three stones).

Summary: A short gully scramble up a roadside crag.

Conditions: The rock is clean and sound, though polished due to its use as a descent route by climbers.

Height Gain: 50m

Approach: The crag is obvious from the A5 (roadside parking here) behind the farm/camp site at Gwern Gof Uchaf (SH 673604) where a well-made path leads to its base.

Ascent: The route follows the obvious deep-cut gully in the centre of the crag. Climb easily up the cleft until below a slightly overhanging chockstone. There are two ways to overcome it: i) it can be taken direct with a struggle, ii) alternatively take a route up cracks on the right followed by a delicate traverse left to step in above the chockstone. Above this, continue more easily up the gully with the sweep of slabs on your left to emerge at the top of the crag.

Usual Descents: Turn right along the top of the crag until grass slopes allow a descent back to its base.

Combinations: The true summit of Tryfan Bach can be reached by turning right and scrambling at grade 3 up a steep groove. Alternatively reach the summit using easy slopes on the left (east) side of this obstacle. Beyond this the best bet is to

make your way on to Heather Terrace that flanks the east face of Tryfan. Here there are numerous scrambles encompassing all grades.

Tryfan Bach Gully Route follows the rocky depression in the middle of the crag

10. Afon Lloer (1) (V)

The best route up Pen yr Ole Wen from Dyffryn Ogwen is undoubtedly the scenic east ridge. The usual way to this is up the path from Glan Dena, but a scrambling approach can be contrived using the Afon Lloer which runs adjacent to the path and drains from the lake of Ffynnon Lloer. It probably doesn't deserve a visit solely on its own merit but if a longer day on the Carneddau is planned it makes a decent start. Ffynnon Lloer itself is extremely sensitive, with *Bryum muehlenbeckii*, *Hedwigia striata*, *Pterigynandrum filiforme* and the *lichen Lecanora achariana*: it is one of the most important lakes in Wales for moss and lichen conservation. The Afon Lloer is less sensitive.

Meaning: Lloer river.

Summary: Easy and escapable scrambling up a stream.

Conditions: The rock is generally sound.

Height Gain: 220m

Approach: From the A5 (roadside parking) at the east end of Llyn Ogwen take a signed footpath north past Glan Dena. The track curves round towards Tal y Llyn Ogwen farm; here take the path that leads off right. Climb a ladder stile and follow the path through a gap in a stone wall before gaining the Afon Lloer (SH 667611) at a small waterfall.

Ascent: Climb the first step centrally then step up onto a small slab on the right side of the stream and dispatch this. Walk up and climb more occasional short falls, keeping to the main right branch. Continue up, making the most of dry streamside rock when it appears. After ascending a wide, easy angled slab (use the runnel/crack on its left) you need to abandon the stream and climb another ladder stile.

Regain the stream bed and scramble up, one entertaining obstacle being several metres of smooth slab on the right of the watercourse. Another notable step features a large quartz block in the stream. When the gradient relents leave the Afon Lloer and take the path on its left. This leads into beautiful Cwm Lloer.

Usual Descents: The path leads beside the stream back to Glan Dena and the A5.

Combinations: The east ridge of Pen yr Ole Wen offers some easy scrambling. Other alternatives are Broad Gully Ridge (1/2), and Craig Lloer Spur (2/3). A pathless way can also be made north toward Rhos Bodesi which sits on the main ridge between Carnedd Dafydd and Carnedd Llewelyn.

Summer evening scrambling on the Afon Lloer

11. Gallt yr Ogof – Cave Gully (1)

Driving from Capel Curig to Ogwen, Gallt yr Ogof looms as a huge bulk of heather and rock; an impressive vision, and a worthy target, until five minutes later down the road and the appearance of Tryfan overshadows its neighbour. Add to this its modest height of 763m, and the result is an unfairly neglected peak. There are climbs recorded on its sprawling north-east face but few bother to visit, and thus the heather rules supreme. The north east face is split by a wide rake/gully that slants from left to right across the crag, which this route takes. The scrambling is poor and short, but the views and atmosphere compensate. Spice can be added to the day by a visit to the cave which gives the mountain its name.

Meaning: Hill of the cave.

Summary: Steep walking up a heathery rake with optional scrambling in a small watercourse.

Conditions: Although the stream generally carries hardly any water, it is best done in a dry spell to avoid the hazards of slippery heather and bracken.

Conditions: In some places the rock of the stream is sound but slimy, but higher up it degenerates into loose rock.

Height Gain: 140m

Approach: Start at Gwern Gof Isaf campsite (SH 685601, car parking at the campsite for a fee) in Dyffryn Ogwen and take the bridleway heading east. A short walk leads below the atmospheric crag, with the rake clearly visible slanting from left to right. Leave the track and walk up to reach it (SH 692595).

Ascent: A steep walk can be had by simply slogging up the rake, and there is a path of sorts. However, scramblers will make the most of rock in the narrow streambed. Most will want to avoid some steps but escape is simple everywhere. Higher up sound rock disappears and walking remains.

The cave itself is clearly visible to the

left of the rake and most will be tempted to visit it. A direct approach is not advised as this involves steep vegetated ground. Instead continue up the rake until a traverse left can be made (there is evidence of other people passing this way) over a heathery bump. Care should be taken (especially in the wet) as although the traverse is just a walk, a slip would deposit the unfortunate adventurer over a nasty drop. I confess that access into the cave may not even be possible. I turned back before the end of the traverse ...

Usual Descents: From the top of the rake a descent can be made west towards the Nant yr Ogof and back to the campsite. A path exists in places.

Combinations: There is a fence and stile at the top of the rake. Cross this to walk the 1km to the summit. From here one option is to head to Y Foel Goch, perhaps descending down the pleasant Braich y Ddeugwm ridge. Another option is to head east over the quiet reaches of Cefn y Capel and down to Capel Curig, returning to the campsite along the bridleway.

David Rider high up in Cave Gully

12. Gallt yr Ogof Slab Route (1 or 2 or 3*)

If any attention is paid to Gallt yr Ogof, it is to the main sprawl of the mountain where the cleanest rock, and the namesake cave, are found. However, on the south side of the Nant y Gors and bordering the left hand side of the cwm lies an area of shallow ribs and slabs. Because of their orientation, they are only visible when passing from Capel to Ogwen; they are hidden when driving the other way. A close investigation reveals that they offer an entertaining scramble on a neglected mountain.

Meaning: Hill of the cave.

Summary: A scramble based upon several slabs/ribs, with a choice of line and difficulty.

Conditions: The rock is clean and sound, though heather intrudes at some points.

Height Gain: 200m

Approach: Approach from the camp site at Gwern Gof Isaf (SH 685601, parking for a fee) and take the bridleway east past the previous route. A gate is reached across the track at SH 695596. Turn right here and follow the wall across boggy ground beneath the cliffs of Gallt yr Ogof. Cross a boulder field and continue across the cwm, hopping the stream of the Nant y Gors to arrive at the base of the slabs/ribs at SH 696588. From below the route can be considered; there are several ribs running up the hillside, and each rib has a slab as its left side. An alternative approach could be made along the same bridleway starting at Capel Curig.

Ascent: A tiny stream runs up to the slabs. Take the slab above it, which is easy angled and is just a walk. Above this the slabs lie at a steeper angle. Move right to the steepest slab, as this offers the best choice of line. Various rising traverses can be made up the slab, or climb to its top and follow the rib along instead (or combine both). If traversing high on the slab the exposure below is not trivial; if following the rib there is one fun knife-edge section with the sweep of the slab on the left and heather on the right.

When the slab/rib ends move left and cross an intermediate rib to gain a vague ridge of rock and heather in a fine position high above the cwm, and follow this until it runs out. Slopes of grass and rock then lead to the eastern ridge of Gallt yr Ogof.

Usual Descents: A descent can be made back into the cwm from Bwlch Goleuni, or the ridge can be followed down over Cefn y Capel to Capel Curig.

Combinations: A short ascent leads to the summit of Gallt yr Ogof. Masochists could then descend Cave Gully, but a pleasant option would be to carry on to Y Foel Goch and descend the Braich y Ddeugwm ridge. Keen and competent scramblers could drop down to Bwlch Tryfan (or down-scramble Bristly Ridge, top end grade 1) and then ascend Tryfan via the South Ridge (grade 1) and descend by the North Ridge or Little and North Gullies on the East Face (both grade 1). The bridleway could then be followed past Gwern Gof Uchaf back to the start.

Dave Jackson on Gallt yr Ogof Slab Route

13. Clogwyn Mawr (1 and 1/2*)

Just behind the Bryn Tyrch Inn at Capel Curig lies the miniature mountain of Clogwyn Mawr ("large cliff"). Its summit clocks in at a lowly 347m but is an exceptional viewpoint. Two scrambles can be had on it; the South Face and the East Spur. The South Face is the steeper and harder of the two. They both serve equally well as a short roadside distraction, or as a prelude to a round of Crimpiau, Craig Wen and Creigiau Gleision (route 14). The height gain for both is approximately 100m on lovely rough rock, and only the briefest of instructions are needed here. There is parking in the village.

South Face (1/2*): Approach using a right of way from either Pinnacle Café or the Bryn Tyrch Inn to the base of the cliff. A good starting point is at SH 728581; just west of where a fence runs up through trees towards the broken cliff is a prominent boulder in the bracken. Go up on pathless ground through the trees to the bottom of the cliff. The start is the steepest and the key to an ascent is finding a rocky and mossy ramp behind some saplings. This slants up right, then back left, before a final step back right gains heathery ground. From here numerous ways up exist, either avoiding difficulties on steep slopes of heather, or seeking out the best of the rock.

East Spur (1*): Approach as for the South Face but this time follow the footpath round to a footbridge at SH 731581. Take a faint path heading north-west and gain the lowest rocks of the low-relief spur. There are countless different route options, and most of the scrambling can be avoided until the summit is reached.

Usual Descents: The East Spur could be used as a suitable descent. Alternatively descend west to a fence then the path back to Pinnacle Café.

Combinations: By heading north some scraps of scrambling can be had, especially just beyond tiny Llyn y Coryn, until Crimpiau is reached. The next route can then be followed.

Approaching Clogwyn Mawr from the west, the South Face scramble is the skyline

14. Creigiau Gleision via Crimpiau and Craig Wen (1***)

At the far end of Dyffryn Ogwen above Capel Curig sits a forgotten little group of hills. The highest top is Creigiau Gleision which broods over the deep Llyn Cowlyd, and just clocks in enough height to be designated a mountain. A round of these peaks from Capel Curig will reward with one of the best views in Wales, with the Carneddau, Glyderau, Yr Wyddfa (Snowdon), Rhinogau and Ffestiniog Hills all in sight. In addition to this, plentiful scrambling can be had on the way for those so inclined.

Meaning: The grey crags, the ridges, the white crag.

Summary: A neglected round of several small peaks offering several sections of scrambling.

Conditions: The rock is mostly clean and sound.

Height Gain: N/A

Approach: There is a car park in Capel Curig. From the village take the path from opposite Pinnacle Stores that heads east past the pinnacles. Beyond Clogwyn Mawr the path veers north-east and skirts marshy ground. Just before it descends to the Crafnant valley (SH 738596, by a wall) a path heads off left; take this. An alternate start involves using the previous route to climb Clogwyn Mawr first.

Ascent: The path winds around small rock walls on its way to the top of Crimpiau, but these provide an early chance to get to grips with rock. Larger walls may require some scouting to find easy lines. Soon, the 475m summit of Crimpiau is reached; a majestic perch at the end of the Crafnant valley commanding superlative-exhausting views of most of Snowdonia's mountain ranges.

From here descend to a path beside a wall that leads below the large rock buttress guarding Craig Wen. This looks fearsome but with a little probing some easier scrambling lines can be found which then bring you to the top of Craig Wen. The way ahead to Creigiau Gleision can now be surveyed; two broken buttresses occupy the centre of the ridge. The main path skirts off to the left but scramblers will tackle both buttresses (Moel Ddefaid and Craiglwyn). Once again the rock is sound and offers a choice of difficulty. Above these it is simply a walk to the main summit of Creigiau Gleision (678m) and its northern top (unnamed on maps, 634m).

Usual Descents: At the end of the summit ridge a fence is met. There are two options: i) Take a path south (marked on the OS map) beside a ruined fence into the forest. A way-marked path then brings you down to Hendre in the Crafnant valley. A right of way then leads back to Capel Curig. ii) Find a faint path through the heather (marked on newer OS map) that drops down to the Llyn Cowlyd dam. A good track on the north side of the reservoir can then be followed back to the A5, just north of Capel Curig.

Combinations: N/A

Below Craig Wen

Dyffryn Ogwen – Further Scrambling Opportunities

There are numerous other streams in the area that offer some degree of scrambling enjoyment. The Afon Wen (grade 1) (SH 675663) on Foel Grach has already been mentioned under the Afon Caseg and Llafar; it is a mossy, disappointing route with little scrambling, but the solitude and atmosphere compensate.

The Afon Berthen drains the huge north-western slopes of Carnedd Dafydd. It runs at a gentle gradient until it turns west and drops down the steep hillside into the Nant Ffrancon. Here a series of cascades and waterfalls have formed that lie hidden from the road. Almost no one notices them, and the situation is not helped by their absence from the OS map. An ascent of the watercourse has the potential to be a pleasant outing of some 150m vertical height (beginning at an unmarked footbridge at SH 636642) but suffers from several problems. Firstly, the interesting part of the stream is on private land. I have never encountered any trouble during my surreptitious investigations but a trip up would still technically be trespassing. Secondly, the woodland surrounding the stream is coniferous and therefore the rocks see almost no sunlight throughout the year, making them potentially very slippery. Thirdly, some of the channel is choked in overhanging vegetation making progress difficult at certain places. This last point could be avoided by an ascent in autumn or winter, but to stick to the line some wading would be necessary and even then some falls may be unclimbable. Perhaps the best bet would be late autumn (afternoon so it would be facing the sun) equipped with secateurs, wet suits and socks worn over footwear! The upper section of the Afon Berthen is also seen to run through a small ravine (around SH 649633) below Carnedd Fach, but closer inspection reveals this to be gentle and uninteresting boulders.

On the western side of the Nant Ffrancon are some interesting streams. Behind Maes Caradoc (SH 635626) is the stream that drains Cwm Perfedd. It runs in a small gorge that may prove interesting, although I have not investigated further. Access land does permit entry, but the farmer may not be too keen on people scrambling up the stream behind his house. On the north side of Cwm Perfedd a rocky ridge is marked on the map (SH 625623), running north-east down to the Nant Ffrancon. From the valley it does not appear as craggy as the map suggests, with the lower section being grassy and uninteresting, but higher up an obvious steepening is seen. Strangely, this obvious ridge is absent from most guidebooks. In reality, it offers a quiet way to the summits with a little easy scrambling. The best approach is to start just south of Tai Newyddion on the old road and ascend steeply to the lip of Cwm Graianog. From here move south to gain the ridge and follow it upwards with excellent views of Carnedd y Filiast's extensive slabs. There are some considerable drops on the right side, but the left is gentle, and the ridge never narrow. It would probably be best as a low grade winter mountaineering route.

Further up the valley is the Cwm Bual Gorge (SH 637621, large grassy area to park at the base). This involves slabby and (mostly) avoidable scrambling in a ravine. Escape is often possible on (sometimes steep) grass, so the route can be done as grade 1. On the first visit we avoided one impossible waterfall by climbing up through a tree in the gorge. Higher up a large, loose cliff rises beside the stream; more reminiscent of some crumbling Spanish gorge.

Above the Cwm Bual Gorge is the chossfest of Esgair Gully. Yr Esgair is the ridge that extends from Foel Goch down towards the Nant Ffrancon. In Scrambles in Snowdonia it was given a grade 3 but described as "thoroughly nasty", "loose and unpleasant" and with an "absence of belay anchors". Unsurprisingly, it receives few ascents, although the lower section of the ridge to the prominent notch is easy walking and scrambling. Esgair Gully climbs up from Cwm Bual to meet this notch, thus giving an excuse to have a look at the fearsome upper ridge of Yr Esgair. Although it is grade I winter, a scrambling grade has little meaning here. Hands seldom touch rock, but instead claw and scrabble against thick moss, loose stones and brown dirt. None of the steps are large but once started escape is impossible (except by retreat) and an unchecked fall could have serious consequences. Nevertheless, the gully is incredibly atmospheric with its twists and turns, and is mercifully short. Just as the adrenaline really gets pumping you emerge out at the notch into bright open air.

On Y Garn there is the Cwm Clyd Gorge (grade 3, SH 638597) that flows into Llyn Idwal. Most of the scrambling is easy enough, but there are two waterfall pitches topped by chockstones that provide the cruxes, and one waterfall that unfortunately cannot be overcome. For those who are repulsed by slime, this is best left alone. It seems that there are scrambling opportunities on the spur that runs south from Llyn Clyd on to the shoulder of Y Garn. This area is known to climbers as Drws Cwm Clyd, and the BMC has agreed to a year-round voluntary ban on climbing here, as it is an important site for arctic-alpine plant species. For this reason, scramblers should refrain from exploring the area.

Just below Idwal Cottage the outflow of Llyn Ogwen drops suddenly down into the Nant Ffrancon valley. When in spate the water races dangerously through two narrow gorge sections, but in summer after a dry spell the waterfalls are less fearsome. A scramble here looks promising, but the waterfalls are home to sensitive bryophytes. *Paraleptodontium, Bryum muehlenbeckii* and a plethora of oceanic species occur on rock faces and the downstream side of boulders. For this reason, scramblers should not contemplate an ascent, and the gorge should be left well alone.

Cwm Idwal is one of the richest botanical sites in all of Wales, and several exceedingly rare flowers grow in the main boulder field (so please don't climb on top of any large boulders). In Cwm Idwal there are several options. One is Nameless Stream; unnamed on OS maps but known as this by climbers. Nameless Stream flows down from Cwm Cneifion to the left of the Idwal Slabs, and when in condition is a grade III ice climb. Out of winter it offers an entertaining scramble for the price of a short and gentle walk in. There are three parallel streams very close together, with the middle channel being the main one. The left hand one is the best choice. From Idwal Cottage take one of the two paths into Cwm Idwal. Proceed along the east shore towards the Idwal Slabs, until the stream is met just before them at SH 645590. The scrambling is good (grade 1) until the route steepens and progress appears blocked by waterfalls, thus necessitating a retreat. The continuation of Nameless Stream in Cwm Cneifion (SH 647588) offers rubbishy scrambling, but escape from the cwm is not easy. I once escaped using the line of Easy Gully (a winter route) and ended up clawing up a nerve-wracking mixture of steep grass, scree, and lichenous loose rock. Not recommended.

Back in Cwm Idwal the bottom section of Idwal Stream (SH 642589) offers some sport. Like Nameless Stream, this is nameless on maps but named by climbers. It is a popular ice climb in winter. It flows down besides the Upper Cliff of Glyder Fawr, and on the right of the Idwal Slabs. The lower section features a relaxed gradient and offers excellent scrambling, with the added bonus of a short walk in and a scenic outlook back over Llyn Idwal. To best appreciate the route, it's a good idea to be prepared to get wet legs and climb all the obstacles direct. I only climbed the route to where it steepens (grade 1 to that point), and retreated from there but it might be possible to ascend the entire stream at a higher grade.

Elsewhere in the area, there are some enticing slabs above Marchlyn Bach reservoir on Elidir Fach. Some of the other mountain gullies may be interesting, such as Red Gully on Foel Goch. Easy Gully (approximately SH 631610) on Foel Goch is the wide fan of rock and scree on the left (south) side of the cwm, and offers a steep way out of the cwm with bits of scrambling.

Y Pàs (The Llanberis Pass)

The Llanberis Pass (known to local shepherds as Y Pàs) rivals Dyffryn Ogwen for its wealth of rock to play on, flanked as it is by Yr Wyddfa (Snowdon) on one side and the Glyderau on the other. The Pass itself is busy most days with boulderers and climbers enjoying the roadside crags, with a fewer number of people venturing further away to the multitude of mountain crags such as Gyrn Las. Huge numbers of walkers also visit to climb Yr Wyddfa from either Llanberis or Pen y Pàs (Pen-y-Pass on the map), though much finer ways to the top do exist.

As would be expected there are plenty of fantastic mountain scrambles such as Crib Goch and the Clogwyn y Person Arête, but there is sport to be had in the gullies, streams and gorges that are sprinkled across the area. The only one that has been described previously is the classic grade 2 of Bryant's Gully which rises up to a spur on Glyder Fawr.

There are camping and bunkhouse opportunities at Nant Peris, as well as youth hostels at Llanberis and Pen y Pàs. Nant Peris is also home to the Vaynol Arms; an excellent place for a pint after a long day on the hill.

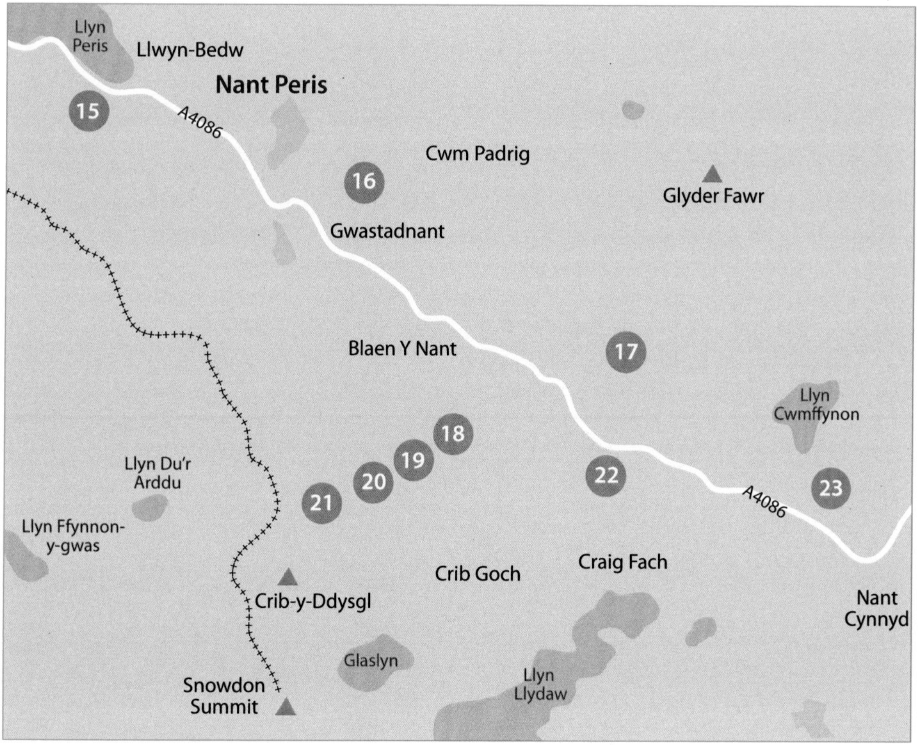
Llyn
Peris
Llwyn-Bedw
Nant Peris
15
A4086
Cwm Padrig
16
Glyder Fawr
Gwastadnant
Blaen Y Nant
17
Llyn
Cwmffynon
18
19
Llyn Du'r
Arddu
20
22
23
21
A4086
Llyn Ffynnon-
y-gwas
Craig Fach
Crib Goch
Nant
Cynnyd
Crib-y-Ddysgl
Glaslyn
Llyn
Llydaw
Snowdon
Summit

15. Clogwyn Mawr Rib (1 or 2)

Above Llyn Peris stands the fractured cliff of Clogwyn Mawr. There is scrambling to be had here, with the described route being selected due to its striking line; a low-relief rib that rises up the hillside. Most obstacles can be avoided on grass on the left, whilst there is occasionally some exposure on the right. This is a good trip to escape the crowds on, and also comes with the advantage of starting virtually at the road.

Meaning: Large cliff.

Summary: Easy scrambling on a narrow rib.

Conditions: The start is loose but on the rib itself the rock is sound. Some sections of the rib are slippery sometimes, particularly towards the top.

Height Gain: 250m

Approach: From the layby at the south end of Llyn Peris climb up the hillside. Cross a fence. The route begins (SH 597587) to the left of some reddish scree and to the left of the building below (Ben's Bunkhouse).

Ascent: Scramble up loose and spiky rock to the base of a short, squat tower. This can be bypassed on the left or right (easier on the right), or climbed directly which proves slightly harder than it looks. From here the line of the rib is more obvious. The next step can be climbed by a groove on the right or by a short chimney on the left.

Continue up to soon reach the crux which shows itself as an innocuous-looking bumpy rise in the rib. This step is quite smooth and with delicate holds. Combined with the drop on the right it is worthy of grade 2. Use the slanting crack on the right and holds to the left of this. To avoid the crux simply leave the rib on the left and walk up past this section.

Beyond this follow the rib up, but be cautious with lichenous rock. Higher up some entertaining technical moves can be enjoyed towards the left of the rib where there is no serious drop. The rib eventually runs out below the minor top of Tryfan.

Usual Descents: A direct descent can be made beside the rib.

Combinations: The ridge can be followed upwards over Tryfan and Llechog to the summit of Carnedd Ugain. Despite the Llanberis Path lying just below this ridge it is seldom walked and gives excellent views across the Llanberis Pass. For a scrambling continuation an approach can be made to Clogwyn Du'r Arddu where the Eastern Terrace offers a grade 1 route up the cliff.

1. *A rainy day on Clogwyn Mawr Rib;*
2. *The view from Clogwyn Mawr Rib.*

16. Afon Las (1 or or 2/3* and 1/2**) (V)

The four branches of the Afon Las ("blue river") originate in Cwm Cneifio, a large, featureless expanse of grassy slopes below Y Garn and Glyder Fawr. This empty solitude is the perfect tonic to the brazen crags and pinnacles of the Ogwen side of the Glyderau, and yet watery thrills can still be found. Two branches are described, and each offers over 300m of vertical height gain. Lower down the scrambling is amongst pretty deciduous trees until open terrain is reached. There are some sensitive bryophyte species on boulders. In summer 2016 a hydropower scheme on the river caused controversy when unsightly tracks were built and large amounts of silt were released into the watercourse. Future developments may render the route description inaccurate.

Parking can be had at Nant Peris or in laybys towards Pen y Pàs, with a road walk to gain the start. Approach using the footpath (SH 615576) from Gwastadnant near Nant Peris. This passes a handful of dwellings before arriving beside the Afon Las, where a gate allows access to the river.

Afon Las Right Hand (1 or 2/3*): Only the crux is worthy of 2/3. Boulder-hop up the river (or walk alongside it), until the first little fall is reached. Climb it on the right away from the water. Continue on, past an island with channels on either side, to where the walls rise up into a small gorge. Here a small fall bars the way: it looks climbable but is guarded by an impassable plunge pool, so avoid it. Hop over a fence and keep on over easy ground. The far left branch enters here, and a bit further on the right branch enters by a stone wall. It is much narrower then the main river.

Low down on the right branch the crux (the grade 2/3 obstacle) is found. It can be bypassed by leaving the gorge. At the back of a narrow slot is a cascade. Climb this, jamming limbs against any wall where security might be found. A brief struggle gives access to a stance and a trap: the only way out is via a second tricky step. Climb it on the right, but be prepared to receive a soaking.

A rocky chicken-run on the right avoids a direct ascent of the next fall, and soon a metal bridge over the stream is reached.

From here the scrambling is more open, with superb views to Llyn Peris, until the walls rise up again and the channel forks, with a spiky spine of rock between the two branches. Either branch can be taken as they rejoin higher up. The rock of the right fork is more crumbly, whilst the left features a hard, avoidable chockstone and is the main channel (and thus is wetter). The two channels rejoin (or rather, the right fizzles out next to the main one) and a slimy fall below a fence is best avoided. Duck under the fence in the watercourse. The scrambling runs for some distance more until the gradient lessens. The path to Llyn y Cŵn lies close by on the left.

The series of terraces on the Afon Las Central Branch

Afon Las Central (1/2**): As for the right-hand to begin with, until that branch departs on the right. From here the stream is wide and bouldery, and the scrambling easy. As height is gained the outlook improves, and the sliminess of the rock lessens. Eventually climb a short rock slab on its right (the stream being at its left). Further on the left branch leaves, and the central branch contains a slightly awkward but avoidable step. Beyond this is an impressive tall waterfall that must be avoided. Leave the stream on the left to escape onto very steep grass, and scrabble up to find a sheep path that traverses right above the waterfall. Above is an optional pool traverse (on the right wall) and a few small steps (note a stone wall on the left).

A steeper, wet step is climbed on excellent rock and the stream opens up into a series of terraces.

Scramble up on clean rock on the left side of the water, with another tall (but stepped) waterfall towering higher up. There is a choice here. The easiest way (in keeping with the route so far) is to escape left along a very slimy ledge with water dripping above. At the end of the ledge squeeze upwards under a propped boulder to emerge on easy ground. The harder option (which increases the grade beyond 1/2) is to continue directly up to the base of the waterfall, accessed via a tight runnel between two boulders. A tricky escape can then be made leftwards at a tree.

A buttress lying on the left side of the

1. & 2. Afon Las Central Branch;
3. The unclimable fall on the Afon Las Central Branch.

stream is the final obstacle. The first step is climbed by a gentle break on its left side (or by a difficult corner decorated with ivy), followed by a few strides left along a vegetated slanted ledge (not for those of a nervous disposition) and a final pull up to easy ground. This can all be avoided using a heathery runnel further left, or completely bypassed by walking left around the buttress. This gains the ground above the waterfall – there is a photogenic promontory directly above the falls for those who enjoy posing. From here the stream hosts a few more steps, or the path can be found over to the right side; cross the stream (very slippery) below a wire fence for convenience.

Usual Descents: The path leads back to the start of the route.

Combinations: A direct slog can be forged to the summit of Y Garn for those who delight in featureless ground and boredom. A grassy descent down Cwm Gafr or the Esgair y Ceunant ridge leads to Nant Peris. Alternatively follow the path onwards to Llyn y Cŵn where a scree treadmill gains Glyder Fawr. The Red Route then leads to Pen y Pàs where a pleasant tramp beside the Afon Nant Peris heads off to the Cromlech Boulders, and a final road walk to the start.

17. South Spur of Glyder Fawr (2)

This route is based on another old Ashton route that was mentioned in early editions of Scrambles in Snowdonia. His route, however, seems to ascend a spur above Pont y Gromlech. Two obvious candidates are visible from the road but neither looks particularly appetising. Instead, the described scramble links several small buttresses further to the left, and runs up to meet the Red Route (the path from Pen y Pàs to Glyder Fawr, so named because of red paint dots on pathside rocks). The route is rather contrived, but the scrambling is good in places.

Meaning: Larger heap/mound.

Summary: A contrived scrambling line over small buttresses.

Conditions: The rock is mostly excellent, though occasionally loose. Due to a lack of traffic heather intrudes in places. As each buttress needs to be spied out in advance this is a route for a clear day.

Height Gain: 450m, but this includes large sections of walking.

Approach: The best place to park is in one of the Cromlech laybys in Llanberis Pass. The route starts at roughly SH 631567. Approach by walking and clambering over boulders (including a stream crossing) to reach the toe of the buttress. Useful recognisable features include a large tree and a dry stone wall next to rock, whilst away to the left the open-book corner of Dinas Cromlech glowers down.

Ascent: The left hand end of the buttress is a vertical wall, with a break to the right (by the tree) perhaps offering a means of upward progression. This route is awkward, however, so instead walk left (past the dry stone wall) and up, and then move right to gain the crest of the buttress. Scramble up on excellent rock with a choice of line, but keep an eye out for a beautiful mini recess of quartz low down. Climb to the top of the buttress, either on the crest (left edge) or on slabs to the right.

From the top of this first buttress look ahead. A shallow, wide 'gully' splits two more buttresses that sit at a relaxed gradient. Aim for the right one, following a faint path in places. This second buttress is heathery, and again offers a choice of line.

Above, a much bigger buttress looms on the skyline. Adventurous scramblers might try to tackle this (perhaps on its left side) but the described route outflanks it. Walk across heather and climb two smaller masses of rock, aiming for the far right end of the skyline buttress. From here the Red Route path comes into view. Don't join it, and instead enjoy some final scrambling on the edge of the large buttress, with some rather steep and hard climbing on offer for those who enjoy a challenge. From here, the views across the Pass and down to Llyn Cwm Ffynnon are superb. By trending left and following the top of the buttress a few more walls can be climbed.

Usual Descents: By joining the Red Route a rapid descent can be made to Pen y Pàs.

Combinations: Walking leads to Glyder Fawr, where a continuation can be made to Glyder Fach and Castell y Gwynt, or Y Garn.

Will Farrelly attempting to find the South Spur of Glyder Fawr

18. Afon Gennog (1*) and the Craig y Rhaeadr Gorge (2**) (V)

Despite being obvious from the road, few people venture into Cwm Glas Mawr. Those that do are often heading to climb on Gyrn Las, or perhaps making their way to the classic scramble of the Clogwyn y Person Arête. The solitude here is breathtaking, yet across the way queues of walkers can be seen inching cautiously along the knife-edge of Crib Goch. The Cwm Glas Ridge bounding the other side of the cwm also merits attention to the discerning walker, yet seldom receives it. Tucked away by the dripping crag of Craig y Rhaeadr an excellent short gorge awaits. When combined with an easy scramble up the Afon Gennog it makes an agreeable start to a longer day on the mountains. Many of the rocks in Cwm Glas are relatively lime-rich, and they provide ideal conditions for an outstanding array of mountain flowers and mosses. Please tread very carefully.

Meaning: Lichen-covered river, the crag of the waterfall.

Summary: Easy boulder-hopping up a stream followed by a more serious scramble up a short but impressive gorge. The final section consists of scrambling up a drier stream.

Conditions: The rock is fairly sound in the Afon Gennog but slime encroaches to some extent in the gorge. The final section is on cleaner rock.

Height Gain: 160m then 100m

Approach: Park in the Llanberis Pass, using one of the laybys down from Pont y Gromlech. Cross a bridge in the Llanberis Pass over the Afon Nant Peris and enter the bed of the Afon Gennog (SH 623568) by the old campsite of Blaen y Nant.

Ascent: Scramble easily up the open stream until you reach a small weir for a hydropower scheme. The river forks, so take the left-hand branch and continue up past a large and smooth boulder that

The steep mossy step in the Craig y Rhaeadr Gorge

occupies the channel. A stone wall follows the left bank here. When the scrambling runs out break away in a roughly south direction aiming for where a stream issues from a dark cleft. This is just to the left of Craig y Rhaeadr; a huge and wet wall of a crag. Proceed up to the start of the gorge (SH 622561).

For those unsure, an easy alternative is to walk and scramble up the right-hand side of the gorge; others can start up the gorge. The first steeper little waterfall is difficult for grade 2, but can be avoided to the right. Above this the water flows through a level trough. This can again be avoided but an entertaining traverse can be made down its left wall.

Now the walls close in and the outlook begins to appear slightly more serious. Climb a steep mossy step to arrive below the biggest waterfall yet; not a chance! A sneaky escape is made here by scrambling out of the gorge on the left side. Turn left again and walk downstream above the gorge until you can make a 180 degree spin and scramble back up to bypass the fall. You can regain the stream here.

A few more short mossy steps are ascended until you reach a vague fork. Take the right branch which proves drier than that below and offers satisfying and more open scrambling. Beyond a flat bouldery area and a few metres of mini-ravine you emerge at a small pool with one final rock step on the other side.

Usual Descents: A descent can be made by moving west and walking down beside the Cwm Glas Mawr Streamway (route 19) which meets the Afon Gennog. This can be followed back to the Llanberis Pass.

Combinations: Crib Goch's North Ridge (grade 1) and Clogwyn y Person Arête (grade 2 or 3) both offer classic scrambling continuations. Another quieter option is to continue to the Cwm Glas Exit (grade 1 – route 21). It is also possible to take a steep scree path from Cwm Uchaf to Bwlch Coch to gain Crib Goch there.

1. The easy rock of the Afon Gennog;
2. Avoiding the big fall in the Craig y Rhaeadr Gorge.

19. Cwm Glas Mawr Streamway (1) (V)

Deeper into Cwm Glas Mawr the cliffs of Gyrn Las block off one escape, whilst further round the terrain rises up in a mass of boulders and broken little buttresses. For those continuing to Cwm Uchaf or Cwm Glas a route through the defences is needed. There are several choices, with this stream offering some easy and escapable scrambling. Although the route is short and mediocre, the views and solitude compensate. As mentioned already Cwm Glas is important for numerous mountain flowers and mosses so care is needed not to disturb the flora.

Meaning: Large green valley.

Summary: Easy scrambling over small steps, followed by a more sustained and slabby upper section.

Conditions: The route is slippery in places, this being more problematic towards the top.

Height Gain: 100m

The Cwm Glas Mawr Streamway offers easy and escapable scrambling

Approach: From Blaen y Nant in the Llanberis Pass follow a path (unmarked on OS maps) on the north side of the Afon Gennog. This leads into Cwm Glas Mawr. Continue until the cliffs of Gyrn Las rise in front of you and you reach a huge quartz-sided boulder. From here head left across pathless ground to reach the stream (SH 618561). Alternatively, the Afon Gennog can be climbed on the approach (see previous route).

Ascent: Scramble up the streambed over assorted easy boulders and steps. Higher up the rock coalesces into water-washed slabs and the climbing is more sustained. Pick a line up this taking care with any wet slippery rock. An enticing variant takes a groove on the left side at the start of this section, before allowing a subsequent return rightwards, but the easiest line keeps to the right. The gradient soon relents and the scrambling ends.

Usual Descents: A descent can be made on the left side of the stream (looking downhill).

Combinations: A short walk brings you to the beautiful Llyn Glas. The Clogwyn y Person Arête (grade 2 or 3) can be climbed from here or the Cwm Glas Exit (grade 1 – route 21) gives an easier escape to Carnedd Ugain's summit. Bwlch Goch can be reached on a steep scree path (good views of Crib Goch from here).

20. The Upper Afon Gennog (1*) (V)

This is the next stream along after the Cwm Glas Mawr Streamway, and drains from Llyn Glas. It is unnamed on new maps but marked as the continuation of the Afon Gennog on the old 1:25000. It offers a more enjoyable route than the previous one, and is harder too. Some falls are best avoided but scrambling on good rock can be had to the side of the watercourse. The rocks of Cwm Glas are relatively lime-rich, and support an array of mountain flowers and mosses, so tread very carefully.

Meaning: Lichen-covered river.

Summary: Good scrambling up a remote stream, and on the rocks that flank it. Many of the steps can be avoided.

Conditions: The route is free from moss. The rock of both the stream and the flanking steps is sound.

Height Gain: 140m

Approach: As for the previous route to the quartz-sided boulder. From here head south to the start of the route at SH 617559. To the left of the stream is a large crag, whilst to the right is more broken ground.

Ascent: As you approach, the first slabby step looks impossible. However, arriving at the base an easy runnel appears on the right and offers a way up. Scramble up to reach another large slab, with the water flowing down its right side. This can be climbed either by a rib on the right (outside of the channel), or up the left side of the slab which features one tricky move to bypass a chockstone.

Above here a few metres of dry scrambling can be enjoyed on rock on the left bank until a point is reached where a large waterfall flows over an overhanging slab. This can be avoided on clean rock outside of the channel on the left (harder) or bypassed over boulders on the right (easier). If the route on the right is taken, a little gorge is entered above the fall;

climb the first step then avoid the next one outside of the stream on the left again.

Just up from here the ground opens out as the gradient relaxes. Walk up to the next rise, keeping with the main (left) channel. Scramble into the gorge under some massive blocks that have peeled off the left hand wall. The stream leads up over small cascades which are best taken on the left, before opening out again. Climb up the centre of another step (likely to get wet here), and then ascend a cracked slab on the left to enter a little runnel/gorge. All that remains now is to traverse along the runnel until the idyllic Llyn Glas suddenly appears.

1. Chris Peacock under the fallen blocks on the Upper Afon Gennog. Remember geologic time is now; 2. Jon McMullin embracing the water; 3. The Upper Afon Gennog.

Usual Descents: A descent can be made back into Cwm Glas Mawr on the west side of the stream.

Combinations: As for the previous route.

21. Cwm Glas Exit (1) (V)

Cwm Glas sits high and remote under the towering peak of Carnedd Ugain; from here it is very much its own mountain rather than a subsidiary peak of Yr Wyddfa (Snowdon). Most of those who make their way into Cwm Glas generally leave by the Clogwyn y Person Arête, or perhaps by Parsley Fern Gully in winter. There is, however, an easy way out on the western side that leads out to the top of the Cwm Glas Ridge. Although the scrambling is scrappy and doesn't last long a trip this way is worth it for the views and the atmosphere alone. A fourth and final mention that Cwm Glas is home to a diverse range of mountain flowers and mosses, and so care should be taken with every footfall.

Meaning: Green valley.

Summary: Scrappy scrambling in a remote cwm.

Conditions: Some of the rock is loose, but it is clean and vegetation is absent.

Height Gain: 120m

Approach: Scrambling approaches can be made via the Cwm Glas Mawr Streamway, Upper Afon Gennog or the Craig y Rhaeadr Gorge. The cwm can also be accessed by walking up the right bank of the Cwm Glas Mawr Streamway or the Upper Afon Gennog. Once in Cwm Glas cross a stream and head to the rocky slopes around SH 615556.

Ascent: To make the most of the scrambling the slope is best examined on the approach. Simply scramble up the numerous small rock buttresses, with a huge choice of line. Most of the rockwork can be avoided by winding around the rock using grass. Be careful with any loose rock. Higher up, the gradient eases but small amounts of scrambling can still be had. Towards the top some scree is found and you soon emerge onto the spur of the Cwm Glas Ridge. A short walk around the top of Cwm Glas brings you to the summit of Carnedd Ugain.

Usual Descents: The Pyg Track and Miners' Track both lead down to Pen y Pàs. The Cwm Glas Ridge (SH 612559) can be

followed back down to Blaen-y-Nant. This involves some scrambling, incuding a short gully (grade 1), before a path leads down (not marked on OS maps).

The Cwm Glas Exit route starts at the lip of the cwm (above and left of the waterfalls) and ascends the rocky shoulder to the ridge

Combinations: For a scrambling continuation a traverse of Crib y Ddysgl and Crib Goch is a classic grade 1 ridge with plenty of exposure. The descent from Crib Goch is then down either the East Ridge or North Ridge (both grade 1).

22. Cwm Beudy Mawr Gorge (1/2)

The Llanberis Pass is streaked with waterfalls and streams that flow from the tops downwards into the tourist-thronged valley. Most probably offer some combination of fear and enjoyment and adventure. This route runs from Cwm Beudy Mawr; the empty space below and between Crib Goch's north and east ridges. Lower down it a gentle stream, yet if persistence is exerted and the watercourse followed then a rocky, gorge-like finale is found.

Meaning: The cwm of Beudy Mawr (farm).

Summary: Easy walking beside a stream, followed by a scramble up a loose and rocky gorge.

Conditions: Lower down the rock is slimy, towards the top it is loose.

Height Gain: 280m (includes walking)

Approach: Start from Pen y Pàs or the layby at Pont y Gromlech. Depending on the start point, walk up or down the road to where the stream crosses at SH 634561. An identifying feature is the dry-stone wall on its right side (looking up).

Ascent: Go through an old gate on the left and walk up beside the stream. By a stone bridge (part of the un-publicised path between Pen y Pàs and Nant Peris) the stream turns left then right again. Branches come in from the left and right but continue vaguely ahead. A short section of scrambling is encountered; the stream flows down a runnel, with a rock slab on the left. You are now in the emptiness of Cwm Beudy Mawr. The silence is paradoxical, with ants silhouetted on the East Ridge of Crib Goch towering above.

Further on, more scrambling can be had on rocks on the left beside the stream, and the channel becomes more incised. Climb two short steps and the gully forks. The left branch is steep and slimy whilst the right is just as repulsive. Take your pick, or valiantly retreat and avoid this section. Above, the stream fades into broken ground. Scramble up on a choice of lines (and some surprisingly good rock) until the stream redefines itself in a rocky gully. Follow this, which gives entertaining but loose scrambling until it finally runs out. More scrambling leftwards over rocky ground leads to the Crib Goch path.

Usual Descents: Follow the path back to the Pyg Track, and from there back to Pen y Pàs.

Combinations: Crib Goch's East Ridge and traverse (grade 1) is the obvious continuation for scramblers, with the option to tackle the entire Yr Wyddfa (Snowdon) Horseshoe. For those who quest in search of less brash thrills, one appealing option is to descend to the Pyg Track, and cross straight over it. A thin, grassy path snakes up to the apparently nameless 609m summit and then past The Horns (named on the OS map) down to Pen y Pàs. Despite being so close to the Pyg and Miners' paths, fellow walkers are rare and the ridge is a rollercoaster of bumpy undulations, which never fail to conjure a good-to-be-alive feeling.

A view down the Cwm Beudy Mawr Gorge

23. Moel Berfedd West Ridge (2*)

Moel Berfedd is a small hill (482m, classified as a Pedwar: a hill of 400-499m with 30m prominence) standing directly above Pen y Pàs and technically belongs to the Glyderau. As it stands at the junction of the Llanberis Pass, Nant Gwynant and Dyffryn Mymbyr it is a superlative viewpoint that asks little effort to reach its summit. As a bonus a short but pleasant scramble can be found on its west side, and when combined with a visit to lonely Llyn Cwm Ffynnon it offers a rewarding hour's diversion.

Meaning: The hill of the middle.

Summary: A short scramble to the summit of a minor hill.

Conditions: The rock is rough and sound.

Height Gain: 120m

Approach: From the car park at Pen y Pàs, cross the road and walk to the left end of the Youth Hostel where a footpath crosses a stile into the garden. Follow this to the end of the garden and the path veers off left. Start here (SH 647557).

Ascent: Scramble diagonally right over large boulders before climbing a short rock step (choice of line). Keep directly up over small steps until the top of the knoll is reached by an aerial, with views of Llyn Cwm Ffynnon and the Glyderau. Look right to see the summit of Moel Berfedd with a rocky ridge taking the right hand skyline: this is the scramble.

Cross a fence by a stile and descend to the base of the ridge. The front of it is steep so reach the crest by scrambling up the side using one of a few different cracks/runnels. Move up the crest on excellent rock with some gentle exposure behind, until arriving at a grassy area backed by a large rock wall. There are several options here. The easiest is to move to the far left end and climb an easy gully/rake. Right again is a harder left-slanting rake. The central area of slab is too difficult for scrambling, but just right of it a third (harder) way up is available. Simple scrambling above this leads to the summit.

Usual Descents: By walking down to Llyn Cwm Ffynnon a path can be picked up back to the Youth Hostel and Pen y Pàs. Alternatively follow the Nant Gwryd across boggy ground until a path can be picked up beside the leat (SH 657561) that leads to a stile just west of the Pen-y-Gwryd Hotel.

Combinations: The nameless stream in Cwm Ffynnon (see Dyffryn Mymbyr – Further Scrambling Opportunities) is the closest nearby scramble beyond the lake, but the Nant Ddu (route 24) can also be reached by moving north-east. A quiet way up Glyder Fawr can be enjoyed by following the 'red route' (so named because paint has been daubed on rocks to mark the way) which is to the west of Llyn Cwm Ffynnon and marked on maps. There is also a faint path that ascends Bwlch Dwyglydion but the country here is reminiscent of the Rhinogau at their worst: uneven ground, hidden rocks and thick heather. For masochists only.

1. *A sunny evening scrambling on Moel Berfedd, above a quiet Pen y Pàs;*
2. *Moel Berfedd West Ridge in profile.*

The Llanberis Pass – Further Scrambling Opportunities

There must be endless entertaining rock in this valley waiting to be documented by keen scramblers. Starting at the far north-western end of the valley is a crag known to climbers as Lion Rocks, which is part of Y Clegyr. This is the name of the craggy dome that sits at the north end of Llyn Padarn. From Craig yr Undeb (and the road to Llanberis) it catches the eye as it protrudes from the lakeside woodland, and invites a closer acquaintance. There is a small car park on the narrow road to Fachwen at around SH 562622. From here a path leads to the crag (a group of new climbers under instruction from an outdoor centre is normally to be found in-situ). The steeper walls are intimidating, but a short scrambling ascent can be made in three distinct sections by using the obvious lines of weakness. The views across to Yr Wyddfa are superb. A descent can be made to the north-east where a little wandering in the forest will reveal the Pine Tree Boulders: an idyllic collection of blocks for a picnic and a spot of bouldering.

Moving away from the main valley, we arrive at the Yr Wyddfa outliers; Moel Eilio, Foel Gron, Foel Goch, Moel Cynghorion. The Moel Eilio to Foel Gron ridge is home to some deep mountain gullies which the brave and intrepid might investigate. Likewise, there is a steep rake at the northern end of the Clogwyn Llechwedd Llo cliff on Moel Cynghorion that attracts and repels in equal measures. Again, a close up look may prove fruitful. In the vicinity is the oddly named "old mantlet" at SH 566569. The National Monuments Record of Wales (NMRW) suggests it may be related to water management or of military use.

Heading up the Llanberis Pass, some falls are marked on the Afon Gafr (SH 611590) and the stream does run in a small gorge at times. The curious may go probing. A little further up again, and it is likely that the two other branches (the left and far left branches – refer to route 16) of the Afon Las at Gwastadnant may offer some sport. The buttress between the far left and left/central branch also looks like it might be an enjoyable scramble. Also at Gwastadnant, but on the other side of the valley, is the Afon Cwm Glas Bach. The Afon Cwm Glas Bach originates in Cwm Hetiau; a place of contrasts. This small cirque is seldom visited, and yet just above clanking trains and an endless stream of tourists head for the summit of Yr Wyddfa. From the Llanberis Pass a few waterfalls are visible on the lower section of river, and higher up an enticing dark cleft can be spied (SH 610567). Despite this the stream is unworthy of attention, as the waterfalls are infrequent. Upon making closer acquaintance with the cleft it becomes apparent that the entry pitch is too steep and slimy. For those that have trudged this far a brief bit of scrambling can be had to the left of the cleft before Cwm Hetiau itself is reached. Access to the ridge is then made either by taking the loose path/scree that slants right to left across the cwm's headwall (used by some doing the 15 peaks), or by moving left to scramble the top section of the Cwm Glas/Gyrn Las Ridge (grade 1). As an aside, access to this side of the valley from Gwastadnant may be dubious. There appears to be no legal access to the bridge from the main road that is used to reach the cottages at SH 613575. Furthermore, although there is access land on the south side of the river, some of this will be 'excepted land'; i.e. the public has no right to access land within 20m of a dwelling, and no access to the curtilage of buildings. Legal access can be gained to the south side of the river by using the footbridge in Nant Peris at SH 604583, where a traverse over rough ground can be made in a south-east direction.

The stream at SH 616558 that links Cwm Glas Mawr and Cwm Glas has numerous small waterfalls in. This is known as Sargeant's Gully to winter climbers. Low down there is easy scrambling until steeper ground begins. The first waterfall can be climbed without excessive difficulty, though a soaking may be had. The next waterfall can be avoided using broken ground on the left, or rock on the right. The third waterfall is also intimidating, and can be bypassed by a vegetated groove on the left. The same pattern repeats above, with steep waterfalls being avoided using rock on the right or vegetated ground on the left, and thus the route makes for a frustrating experience and is best avoided. Just over

Garnedd Ugain is the stream (SH 614546) that flows into Glaslyn. In its lower reaches it is steep, although it appears mostly escapable.

On the northern side of the Llanberis Pass is Bryant's Gully; a long scramble in three sections, graded 2 or 3 depending whether you use "Scrambles in Snowdonia" or "North Wales Scrambles" There are probably other streams on the same side of the Pass that may provide some scrambling.

1. Finding a way round waterfalls in Sargeant's Gully; 2. Investigating the scrambling potential of Lion Rocks.

2

Dyffryn Mymbyr

Dyffryn Mymbyr is the short valley that links Capel Curig with the Pen-y-Gwryd Hotel. It is flanked on the north by Glyder Fach, Glyder Fawr and Y Foel Goch, and on the south by Moel Siabod.

In contrast to the valleys of the previous two chapters, there is little continuous rock or fearsome drama here. Instead, a wide sense of space and emptiness prevails. Despite the lack of rock, two scrambles of interest can be found within the valley, and two more on Moel Siabod can be approached from here (refer to the Glyn Lledr chapter for these).

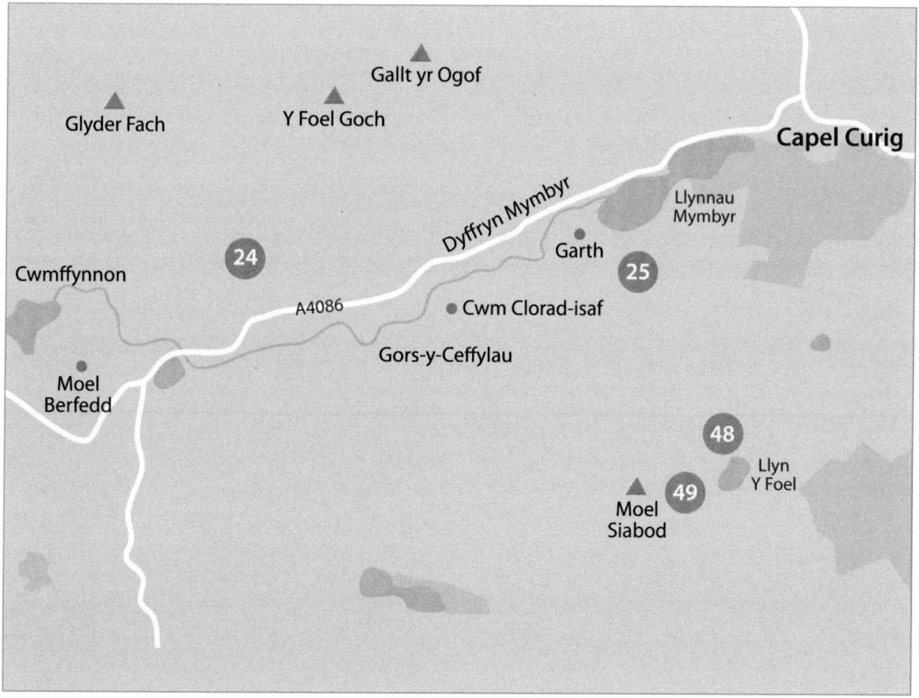
Gallt yr Ogof
Glyder Fach
Y Foel Goch
Capel Curig
Llynnau
Mymbyr
Dyffryn Mymbyr
Garth
24
25
Cwmffynnon
A4086
Cwm Clorad-isaf
Gors-y-Ceffylau
Moel
Berfedd
48
Llyn
Y Foel
49
Moel
Siabod

24. Nant Ddu (1**)

What's this; a worthwhile scramble on the southern slopes of the Glyderau? It certainly is! The Nant Ddu rises for some distance up the side of Glyder Fach and provides entertaining grade 1 scrambling up an open streambed. Because of its grade and ease of escape it would make a reasonable introduction to the sport. It is also a much better alternative than walking up the Miner's Track which is used to access this side of the mountain.

Meaning: Black stream.

Summary: Solid grade 1 scrambling up an open streambed.

Conditions: Slime is present on wet rock, but much of the scrambling is on clean rock too. The rock quality itself is very good.

Height Gain: 270m

Approach: There is roadside parking near the Pen-y-Gwryd Hotel. The scrambling starts at SH 669568, just above the stone wall. This can be approached directly from the road below by following the lower stream. Alternatively, if starting at the Pen-y-Gwryd Hotel cross the stile that leads to the Miner's Track then immediately move right (north-east) across wet ground. Various sheep paths and the occasional faint vehicle track can be followed towards the start of the route. Interestingly, there are several wooden signposts in the area; the remains of a path from the Pen-y-Gwryd to Capel Curig, known as the Esme Kirby Path.

Ascent: Start at SH 669568 just beyond the stone wall. The first obvious barrier to progress is a narrow pool backed by a wall. It might be possible to traverse either wall, but overhanging gorse and heather intrude. It could be avoided altogether but this seems a shame. The best solution then, is to wade the pool and climb the short back right wall on clean rock and good holds. The next waterfall is much bigger and unfortunately cannot be climbed, so bypass it on the left. Another less steep waterfall then presents itself;

climb this on dry rock on the right and continue up.

Above is an easy-angled chute which can be climbed on its left side and with the use of grippy quartz in the water. Next are numerous small steps until a larger fall is again reached. Dispatch it on its left side with a tricky final move (the holds are there if you reach) then climb a slabby chute. From here it's simply a case of keeping upwards, with plenty of entertaining steps to enjoy until the gradient lessens and rocky craglets appear ahead. Shortly the place is reached where the Miner's Track fords the stream. Ignore the path and climb one final larger waterfall (best taken just left of the middle) to finish.

Usual Descents: The nearby Miner's Track can be followed back to the Pen-y-Gwryd Hotel.

Combinations: A path to the right of the stream leads faintly north across the boggy area to meet the main path between Y Foel Goch and Glyder Fach. From here you can head east or west over various tops.

A dreich day on the Nant Ddu

25. Creigiau'r Garth Gorge (1*)

Behind the much-photographed twin lakes of Llynnau Mymbyr the slopes of Moel Siabod rise up in an expanse of heather, grass and rock. Apart from groups of students from Plas y Brenin practising their navigation few venture onto the lower slope. For gorge scramblers, however, there is an incentive in the form of a stream that cleaves the craggy Creigiau'r Garth. It is not obvious on the map (except in the marking of 'falls') but the gorge is visible from the road between Capel Curig and the Pen-y-Gwryd Hotel. This is a route recommended for those after something accessible but slightly lonely, with new views of Dyffryn Mymbyr.

Meaning: Garth (farm) rocks.

Summary: Bouldery scrambling up a square-cut gorge, followed by short falls in a more open landscape.

Conditions: Being north-facing the rocks are very slippery in places.

Height Gain: 140m

Approach: There is roadside parking just west of Plas y Brenin (Capel Curig). Take the footpath south past the Plas y Brenin and over the bridge at the eastern end of Llynnau Mymbyr. The footpath up Moel Siabod goes straight ahead here, but instead turn right along a forest track. Where the track ends, a small path takes over and weaves through the trees to a fence at the edge of the forest. Cross the fence and continue heading in the same direction above the lake. There are several faint paths that weave through the bracken. At SH 704568 a fence and walls are reached. Cross these to meet the stream.

Ascent: Walk up the stream on the right to meet a bold slab. Most will not want to tackle the lower section as it is quite featureless, so walk up on the right and use grassy lumps to enter a crack in the slab halfway up (perhaps grade 2). Above, scramble up dry rock on the right of the stream then clamber over boulders to a wall at the bottom of the gorge.

Climb a slimy ramp on the right and

pick a line up until a larger fall is reached. Avoid the water by using rocks on the right and keep up over assorted obstacles. At one point, escape can be made by exiting the gorge via a ramp of grass and quartz on the left. More scrambling (often taken on the far right or left to get the driest rock) leads to a long ramp where the water flows down the middle. Climb this, then another little boulder blockage to reach open ground. More scrambling can be had on small waterfalls until, after a flat section, a slabby wide fall is reached. A direct ascent is impossible, but the step can be climbed on the far right, with good holds to top out. The scrambling peters out beyond.

Stuart Gillies in the Creigiau'r Garth Gorge

Usual Descents: Further up a fence is reached. This can be followed north-east to pick up the path back to Plas y Brenin.

Combinations: After reaching the path (as for the descent) it can be followed to the summit of Moel Siabod. Alternately, another fence (unmarked on OS maps) can be followed in a hard slog directly up the slope that eventually reaches the Moel Siabod path by twin ladder stiles. From the summit a descent can be made down the west ridge, or the easy grade 1 ridge of Daear Ddu (route 49) can be taken on the south side of the mountain.

Dyffryn Mymbyr – Further Scrambling Opportunities

For the most part this isn't a particularly rocky valley, and so the scrambling potential is limited. There is a watercourse that tumbles down from Gallt yr Ogof and crosses the road at SH 690568, by the farm track to Cwm Clorad Isaf. It provides some scrambling (grade 1) but nothing exceptional, and the falls are quite slimy. Interestingly, a faint path escorts the stream in its lower wanderings. Higher up the stream shrinks in size, so move left to cross a wall and gain a second stream at SH 687573. Higher up beyond another wall there are the remains of several dwellings. At the same point on the other side of the valley is an interesting looking slab with a crack in it (around SH 696563), and an easy-angled stream to the right of it. Both may be worth a look, though access would be tricky. The access land on either side of the river is separated by non-access land where the track to Cwm Clorad Isaf bridges over the Nant Gwryd. A rough approach would have to be made from Capel Curig or by way of access land in the vicinity of Gors y Ceffylau. Be warned, last time I was here I couldn't find the stepping stones that the OS map claims exist and had to ford the river (icy!). Even if the slab and stream disappoint, Cwm Clorad is a worthy place to wander. I find it has a

melancholic atmosphere, scattered with stone ruins (although Gors y Ceffylau shows signs of occasional habitation; when I last passed it was locked, but an outbuilding was stocked with toilet roll).

There is another diverting scramble on the south flanks of the Glyderau, below Glyder Fawr. Behind Llyn Cwm Ffynnon at SH 646570, just below where the hillside steepens, is an open and easy-angled but slabby stream. It offers rather unique slabby scrambling of a technical nature, perhaps grade 2 but completely escapable. After one steep step the narrow stream forks. The left branch entices with a gentle gradient and a beautiful line of narrow waterslide slabs rising up, which deteriorate into rubbishy scrambling higher up. The height gain is about 130m.

1. The narrow slabby stream in Cwm Ffynnon; 2. A winter view down Dyffryn Mymbyr.

Nant Gwynant

Nant Gwynant shows yet another side to Snowdonia. Its lower slopes are green and wooded, reflected in the picturesque lakes of Llyn Gwynant and Llyn Dinas, whilst the summits above, such as Cnicht and Moel Meirch are wild and untrodden.

The area lacks the wealth of classic mountain scrambling found in Dyffryn Ogwen and the Llanberis Pass, but this is compensated by some excellent adventures in the streams, gorges and gullies that line the valley. The Afon Merch, in particular offers one of the best days out to be had in this book, whilst the Afon Goch is a useful introduction for those new to the delights of gill scrambling.

The A498 runs through the valley, and a base in Beddgelert at the south eastern end is probably most convenient. The northern end of Nant Gwynant also makes a good destination to end a day on the hill, as it is home to the excellent, and historic, Pen-y-Gwryd Hotel.

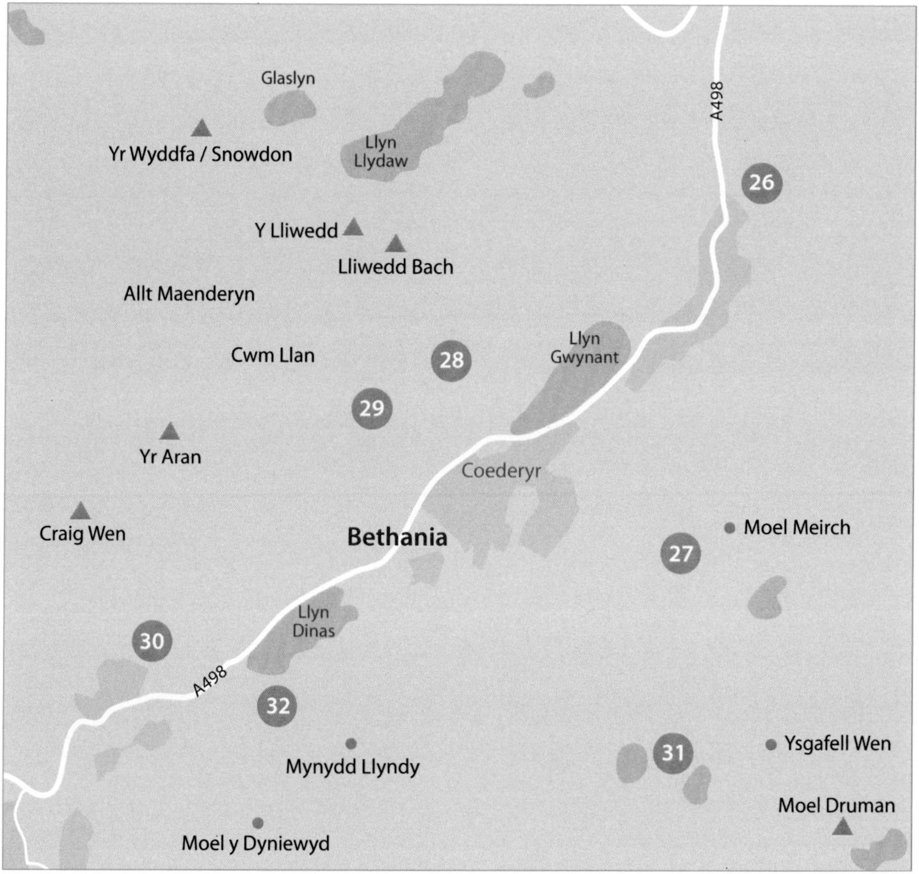
Glaslyn
Yr Wyddfa / Snowdon
Llyn Llydaw
A498
26
Y Lliwedd
Lliwedd Bach
Allt Maenderyn
Cwm Llan
28
Llyn Gwynant
29
Yr Aran
Coederyr
Craig Wen
Bethania
27
Moel Meirch
Llyn Dinas
30
A498
32
Mynydd Llyndy
31
Ysgafell Wen
Moel Druman
Moel y Dyniewyd

26. Ceunant Mawr (2*)

Just after passing the viewpoint and car park on the road from the Pen-y-Gwryd to Beddgelert, the base of the Ceunant Mawr gorge is passed. This is a gorge for the impatient – it lies about 400m from the car park.

Meaning: Big ravine.

Summary: The scrambling in the lower gorge is easy. Higher up the stream runs through a narrow slot and two tricky traverses are needed to gain easier ground above.

Conditions: The rock in the open lower gorge is mostly good, but higher up more slime is found.

Height Gain: 150m

Approach: Park at the car park/viewpoint at SH 658541 and walk south down the road until a bridge is reached at the base of a large ravine at SH 659537 (don't confuse this with the lesser stream of the Ceunant Ifan which is crossed first).

Ascent: Leave the road and gain the right bank, noting an old mine adit on the left, and a rock with various graffiti marked into it on the right. At first the scrambling is poor, and some steps must be avoided on the right, but the environment soon opens out. Boulder hop upwards until a waterslide is reached. Traverse in on the left then climb the slide, with the view of the Snowdon Horseshoe behind constantly improving with height. The next optional interesting section is found at a large square(ish) boulder in the centre of the stream. Pass this using slippery ledges on the left bank.

More bouldery scrambling then leads to the most interesting section yet. In some trees the stream, backed by a short fall, flows along a deep, narrow trough; time to take stock of the situation. Escape is made by traversing the left wall. There is a small ledge for feet that starts off being rather thin but becomes more comforting further along. Handholds can be found but most are on the small side. Socks over boots for extra grip are recommended here. Once at the other end the short fall

yields easily to reveal another pool. This time the right wall is traversed rather awkwardly, using some submerged ledges to start before a shelf is gained. Climb the fall above using the rocky ramp on the left.

Above, another pool is reached with no possible traverse, so climb out on the left side onto grass. The gorge opens up into a pleasant environment of trees and grassy slopes. Straightforward scrambling leads up to where a large waterfall cascades down the right hand wall: a refreshing place in hot weather. Continue up the bouldery gorge until two final short falls are climbed. Beyond the gorge is smaller. Traverse a horizontal section and soon the stream subsides into grassy moorland. At last the interesting grey rock of the area (found in the adjacent gorges) reveals itself.

Mark Cooper in the Ceunant Mawr, showing the first tricky traverse (photo 3)

Usual Descents: Slopes can be descended on the north side of the gorge directly to the road. If it can be found an old tramway is a useful guide. It is the remains of a route between the Cwm Dyli Power Station and Garnedd in the Lledr Valley.

Continuations: Carnedd y Cribau can be ascended by pathless going. For determined scramblers, head to Moel Meirch or the Afon Merch or Afon Cwm Llan (routes 27, 28 and 29).

27. Moel Meirch (1 or 2 or 3*)

Any connoisseur of the quiet places of Snowdonia should be on familiar terms with Moel Meirch ("the hill of horses"). It is a sprawling badland of boggy ground, rocky craglets and wild heather above Nant Gwynant. It is sometimes climbed as part of a logical traverse from Moel Siabod to Allt Fawr or Cnicht, but rarely done on its own, being a few metres short of mountain status. Despite this it is a worthy target.

Meaning: Hill of horses.

Summary: Pick 'n' mix scrambling up a range of slabs and mini buttresses.

Conditions: The rock quality is mostly good.

Height Gain: 200m, including walking.

Approach: It is best climbed from Bethania or from the narrow lane that leads to Hafodydd Brithion at SH 639494 if buses aren't being used; there is limited parking at SH 635496 but more along the road towards Gelli Iago. Take the right of way past Hafodydd Brithion towards the Afon Llyn Edno, which is delightful company on the ascent, particularly when the rhododendrons are in flower, and the gorge at SH 649499 offers a short scramble.

Ascent: From the Afon Llyn Edno, break out onto the western slopes of Moel Meirch where a plethora of small slabs and crags offer endless scrambling potential. Don't come solely for the scrambling; come for the solitude and the wildness, and enjoy the ad hoc scrambling as a bonus. This is a hill best left for a sunny day, for when you tire of clambering on the rocks, head to nearby Llyn Edno. This is an idyllic spot, and the perfect location for a cooling swim.

Usual descents: A right of way heads back down from between Moel Meirch summit and Llyn Edno, though it can be tricky to find this on the ground.

Combinations: It would be possible to

The wild lands of Moel Meirch

descend north to Bwlch y Rhediad and then somehow contrive a way across to the Daear Ddu Ridge (route 49) on Moel Siabod, but this would be a bit of a slog. Better to wander north to Carnedd y Cribau, or south to Ysgafell Wen and Cnicht. Numerous descents are then possible.

28. Afon Merch (2 or 3***)

Bethania sees its fair share of people; those fed up with the usual routes up Yr Wyddfa (Snowdon) come here to walk the Watkin Path. Hidden from view in the woods behind Hafod y Llan is an even more scenic attraction. The Afon Merch is a lengthy stream that tumbles down from Cwm Merch below Lliwedd and Gallt y Wenallt. In its lower course it runs over waterfalls surrounded by delightful woodland, whilst its upper reaches consist of more cascades situated in a forgotten and un-walked cwm. The Afon Merch makes an excellent long scramble, and is a highly recommended way to gain the mountain tops.

Meaning: River of the young maiden.

Summary: A long scramble through beautiful surroundings. All difficulties are avoidable and most are escapable. Apart from the crux the route makes a pleasant and easy grade 2.

Conditions: The rock is surprisingly clean and generally sound.

Height Gain: 400m

Approach: There is a car park at Bethania, but access to the stream is a bit tricky. Note that the lower part of the gorge (up to where the stream forks at SH 629516) is not access land but is owned by the National Trust. The suggested approach is to take the Watkin Path from Bethania until it curves left and overlooks the Afon Cwm Llan. Go down off the path here – this isn't access land but is rough ground, and plenty of people seem to wander about – cross the river to locate a gate into the woods where access land begins. Walk through the woods below Clogwyn y Barcut to reach a fork in the river (SH 629516).

Ascent: There are two channels of the Afon Merch at the start (marked on the OS map) so take the right one (the left one also goes, but the scrambling is perhaps less good). Scramble easily up until you reach a much larger fall. Pick a dry line up this and continue through lush, green surroundings until you reach an evil-

looking dank ravine. It is possible to traverse a little way along this cleft but an exit would be nigh on impossible (it would involve swimming and a difficult subterranean ascent), so move right before the ravine and walk along the bank before regaining the stream bed.

Carry on up the stream, traversing deep blue pools and climbing small cascades. Pass a tree in the middle of the rocky channel and soon arrive at another steepening. This can be easily climbed up the centre, or if a challenge is wanted take the left-hand channel with a short traverse

Adam Pearce on the upper Afon Meirch

and tricky exit (but beware the large slab that follows as it lacks holds).

Higher up another pool beckons. Traverse around this and scramble up the waterfall on its easier-angled left side. Enter a narrow slot which ends at a steep waterfall. This is the crux (harder than grade 2) but if you have any doubts you can leave the narrow slot before the fall and avoid this step. To overcome the crux, start up the left-hand side on slippery holds to gain a stance a few metres up. From here exit left with an ungainly mantelshelf/thrutch move.

The trees now thin out and the gradient lessons. Walk up the channel with occasional short steps. Eventually a stone wall appears on the right then switches to the left bank, and a small tributary enters on the right. Carry on until confronted by a large and intimidating square wall of about 6m height. Despite its appearance an ascent of this is without complication and equipped with good holds. The next cascade is also overcome with ease by a choice of lines.

The view ahead opens out once more and a large succession of waterfalls can be spied further up. These offer good

1

scrambling on sound rock, provided the slimy sections are avoided. Beyond these falls, the stream meanders across a level section and enters another small gorge. This can be entered from the right or with a traverse on the left (beware any gorse!). Traverse the left wall of the pool ahead then bypass the next slimy fall on its right

1. *Climbing the 'square wall'*; 2. *Michèle Oakley in the lower Afon Merch.*

turns left and climbs up to the copper mines below Y Lliwedd where it peters out.

Usual Descents: An old miners' path (marked on the OS map) leads back to Bethania.

Combinations: Lliwedd can be ascended by something of a slog. A more agreeable option is to head to Gallt y Wenallt. Walk up through the mines until you reach a fearsome quarried cleft in the rock. Here look right where a faint path breaks away across the slopes to bring you out onto the ridge just before the 619m summit. A worthwhile descent from here is then down the north-east ridge; a narrow grassy arête.

side. Around the corner proceed along a narrow trough and re-emerge into open flat ground.

From here upwards the scrambling is mostly simple, but there is more slime on the rock. One larger fall is more straightforward than appearance suggests from a distance. Eventually the stream

29. Afon Cwm Llan (1**)

The Afon Cwm Llan is the river that escorts the Watkin Path in its lower wanderings as it climbs towards Yr Wyddfa (Snowdon). Like its neighbour; the Afon Merch, it consists of clear blue pools, scenic cascades and entertaining scrambling. The difference in the two is popularity. Due to the proximity of the Watkin Path the stream is busy on hot sunny days with people paddling, swimming and sunbathing. Despite this, it makes a good morning start to a long day on the tops.

Meaning: Cwm Llan river.

Summary: Easy and escapable scrambling up a beautiful river.

Conditions: The rock itself is excellent. The first main fall is slimy, but higher up the scrambling focuses on dry clean streamside rock.

Height Gain: 120m

Approach: From the car park at Bethania follow the well built Watkin Path (signed) through attractive woods. It passes through two gates before the view opens out at a corner above the Afon Cwm Llan. Descend on grass to reach the river around SH 627513.

Ascent: Here the river consists of several channels so pick a way up, walking with a few scrambly steps until the river flows across flat ground. Walk beside the stream until the first big fall is reached. This first fall is quite slippery with slime, and the best grip is to be had on the clean water-washed rock. The first few feet can be climbed on rock on the far right before switching across to more clean rock on the left. Above this first fall a stone bridge crosses the watercourse and the route reveals its true character.

Traverse under the bridge on the left above blue water of a stunning clarity. A waterfall presents itself beyond a deep blue pool. This is a tempting place for a swim on a hot day, with a convenient slanted slab beside the water to sunbathe on. To continue, take the right bank and step around a wooden fence. Although the waterfall first looks intimidating it is easily climbed on the right to reveal yet another idyllic swimming pool. Traverse this on shelves on the right, passing a tree and ducking under a holly bush.

From here keep on up, taking steps on either side of the stream. The hardest obstacle is a wet slab on the left side. This involves traversing a short easy groove, before climbing up a few feet, moving along, and then descending a few feet to a second groove. After dispatching more excellent streamside rock, old mine buildings appear on the right and a wall is climbed on the left. The Watkin Path is adjacent to the stream here, and so any scramblers often have an audience. Most people will leave the stream here, as the next fall is taken by traversing in from the right, but involves a few metres of swimming (or a foolhardy leap!).

Usual Descents: The Watkin Path leads back to the start. There is a more scenic path on the other bank, however, that leads back to the stone bridge.

Combinations: The Watkin Path can be followed up to the summit of Yr Wyddfa (Snowdon). Alternatively, a faint path can be followed that leads onto the east ridge of Yr Aran. Another fine option is to follow the old tramway to Bwlch Cwm Llan where the excellent south ridge of Yr Wyddfa leads up to the summit. Scramblers have four options. From Bwlch Cwm Llan some limited rock is available on the north ridge of Yr Aran. Another option is the neglected grade 2 Tregalan Couloir on the flank of Yr Wyddfa's south ridge. Finally, and perhaps most pleasingly, the Watkin Path can be followed to Bwlch Ciliau. From here some scrappy grade 1 scrambling can be found on the east ridge of Yr Wyddfa, but the better option is to traverse Lliwedd and enjoy some excellent grade 1 scrambling to the airy summit. After this, a walk on to Gallt y Wenallt will shake the crowds of the Yr Wyddfa Horseshoe. There are two descents; one down the south-east ridge back to Bethania, or one down the airy grass arête of the north-east ridge, over the top of the Afon Glaslyn gorge and down to the Afon Trawsnant. A right of way then heads south back to Bethania.

Sun-drenched streamside rock on the Afon Cwm Llan

30. Afon y Cwm (1/2)*

The Afon y Cwm is a sister river to the Afon Merch and Afon Cwm Llan. All three sit on the same side of Nant Gwynant within a few miles of each other, and share the same mix of deep, blue pools and enjoyable scrambling. The Afon y Cwm is found behind the National Trust property of Craflwyn, and is the least enjoyable of the three, although still worthwhile.

Meaning: River of the cwm.

Summary: Open scrambling up a stream, featuring scenic pools and waterfalls. Escape is always easy.

Conditions: The rock quality is good but slime does intrude at some points. Often, the water-washed rock provides the best grip.

Height Gain: 100m

Approach: There is free parking and toilets at a National Trust car park at SH 599489, where an information board shows the permissive paths around the grounds of Craflwyn. Walk down the access road to Craflwyn Hall and onwards, to reach a blue pool and waterfall on the Afon y Cwm at SH 603493.

Ascent: Avoid the first fall by scrambling up mossy rocks on the left side. Next up is a short, steep waterfall of a few metres, well-equipped with holds. Above this the view opens out, and a series of cascades are seen ahead. The top cascade can be climbed on either the right or left side, but the right side may be preferable as the left ascent leads on to an easy-angled but rather slippery slab. The view back to Mynydd Sygyn keeps improving with height. The next notable feature is a very deep pool backed by a waterfall. It seems feasible that a route might exist up the dry right hand rocks, but the first few steps from the pool-side ledge would be the hardest, and so it is best to leave the stream on the west side (by four water tanks) and avoid this fall. The next major obstacle is another pool and short waterfall, tackled on the left with a step down to bypass the pool, and a scramble up slippery rock. Further up is more wading and scrambling, followed by a flat, uninteresting section of ground where the stream channel splits in two to flow around a sliver of land. Around the next corner is an easy traverse on the right side of a pool and a final simple step.

Usual Descents: It is possible to follow the stream bank back towards Craflwyn Hall, perhaps breaking off in a south-western direction from near the water tanks and descending to the bottom of Ffos y Gelli, the next stream along to the west.

Combinations: From nearby a permissive path runs over to the Watkin Path up Yr Wyddfa (Snowdon), where the Afon Cwm Llan and Afon Merch (routes 28 and 29) both offer good scrambles. Alternatively, it would be possible to forge a way up to the hill of Gallt y Llyn or even Yr Aran.

Tom Hecht in the Afon y Cwm, including the waterfall that must be bypassed (photo 2)

31. Craig Llyn Llagi Gorge (1/2**)

This is a minor classic – the dank, vegetated cliffs of Craig Llyn Llagi are cleaved on their left side by a stream that tumbles down a gully. This is visible from quite a distance, and looks very intimidating. In actual fact, appearances can be deceptive, and the stream offers an excellent approach to Cnicht, Ysgafell Wen or Moel Druman. The scrambling is mostly easy and enjoyable, and the view back over Llyn Llagi to Yr Wyddfa (Snowdon) and friends is breath-taking on a good day.

Meaning: Unknown.

Summary: Bouldery scrambling up a mountain gully/stream.

Conditions: The rock is quite slippery, and care should be taken with any loose blocks.

Height Gain: 160m

Approach: A footpath leaves the minor road from Bethania to Nantmor at SH 635490. Do not park here. There is some space to park at SH 635496, and a small car park down the road at Gelli Iago. However, my preferred approach is from the car park at Bethania, though this adds an extra mile and a half or so. From the car park take the private road (footpath signed) through Plas Gwynant. On a warm morning this is a delightful start, with birds calling in the woods. The path leaves the road on the right, and crosses the Afon Llyn Edno before meeting the minor road to Nantmor. Walk along the road – this is no chore, as traffic is infrequent and the views excellent. Shortly after the road makes a sharp right turn the footpath at SH 635490 is reached.

Follow this as it passes left of the house of Llwyn yr Hwch, and over a stile near a waterfall. The path is vague in places as it dodges the occasional outcrop or bog, but after a mile it reaches Llyn Llagi. The route is obvious. Pass to the left of the lake (very boggy) to reach the walls at the base of the stream (SH 651483).

Ascent: Start up, or beside the stream. At first escape is easy, until higher up the gully walls rise up and the only exit is to retreat or continue. The scrambling is mostly bouldery until the crux is reached. There are three options: 1) Go far left and climb an easy-angled but slimy slab, lacking in good holds, 2) Climb directly up the water (easier in the dry), or 3) Move far right and climb a short step in the corner. Beyond this is more clambering with a choice of line.

Eventually a larger cascade is reached. The timid can escape below this on the right and bypass it on a loose path. The best option is to go right up to the base of the waterfall. From here, traverse right on a horizontal break, then up and back left with a touch of (welcome?) exposure. A few more steps then lead to the top.

Usual Descents: By heading left (north-east) a path can be joined that descends back to Llyn Llagi.

Combinations: Cnicht is a worthy objective from here, perhaps followed by a short down-scramble south-west off its summit, and a descent to Gelli Iago (where another gorge is found – see further scrambling opportunities). For those more interested in solitude and contemplation, then Ysgafell Wen and Moel Meirch will make suitable companions.

Looking out from the Craig Llyn Llagi Gorge

32. Afon Goch (Llyn Dinas) (1***)

The Afon Goch drains a minor catchment to the north of the small hill of Moel y Dyniewyd. It flows over numerous small falls before entering Llyn Dinas at its south-west end. It provides good easy scrambling through a pleasant (if unnatural) landscape of short conifers and rhododendrons. The route begins mere minutes from the road and so is a good choice if pressed for time.

Meaning: Red river.

Summary: Easy and escapable scrambling up a scenic stream.

Conditions: The rock is quite sound. Some slime is present but this presents no problems.

Height Gain: 100m

Approach: From the A498 take a path at the western end of the lake (parking is available here). Cross a footbridge over the Afon Glaslyn and continue along the lakeside path until it fords the Afon Goch (SH 614492). This is the route.

Ascent: Start up the stream (or on the bank if preferred) until small cascades present themselves. These are dispatched with ease. The first major obstacle is an obviously larger and steeper fall. Climb the lower section on the left before crossing the water to scramble up the right with a slight increase in difficulty.

Continue upwards in delightful surroundings over more small steps until you reach the crux. This is another larger fall split into two sections. A direct ascent is best ignored so overcome the lower part using a runnel on the far right. The upper step can then be climbed on the right or left side of the water, with the left generally being wetter.

This is the end to most of the fun, although a wall flanking the right side higher up offers an entertaining traverse of a few metres. When ready abandon the watercourse and walk west to find a large path.

Usual Descents: This path can be followed back down to Llyn Dinas.

Combinations: A short day can be had by climbing Moel y Dyniewyd (382m) and Mynydd Sygyn (300m), perhaps combined with a walk back along the Pass of Aberglaslyn. A mediocre scrambling option is nearby on Yr Arddu, and the gorge at Gelli Iago offers slightly better sport (see further scrambling opportunities for information on both), or a more strenuous day can be had by heading to Cnicht, with the option of another scramble on Craig Llyn Llagi (route 31).

Pete Early on the Afon Goch (Llyn Dinas)

Nant Gwynant – Further Scrambling Opportunities

Nant Gwynant has plenty more to offer the dedicated gorge explorer. Starting at the head of the valley is the mighty gorge of the Afon Glaslyn itself. At SH 649543 it tumbles down from Cwm Dyli in a short, steep gorge. I've never entered the gorge itself and an ascent would almost certainly be hard, but it might be possible in dry weather. Perhaps someone braver than I can try it?

On the east side of the valley is a nameless gorge (SH 658531) just down from the Ceunant Mawr. It is visible to passing motorists as a green and fecund hanging garden, choked with wild garlic and primroses in spring. An ascent is possible, grade 1, with 100 m of poor scrambling. However, it is probably best left alone in its glorious green and overgrown state. Just appreciate it from the road. A little way down the valley again is the Afon Feingam (SH 658527). This is another 'lost world' style ravine. The name translates as something like "narrow crooked river". This may be due to the nature of the curious grey rock that dominates the stream, also seen at the top of the Ceunant Mawr. There is perhaps 140 m of scrambling at grade 2, with one larger waterfall providing the crux. Like the previous route it is probably best left alone to allow the wild and overgrown conditions to prevail. The scrambling is not of great quality, so it is no great loss.

Moving down Nant Gwynant further (and off into a side valley) we find a gorge behind the Nantmor Mountain Centre at Gelli Iago (SH 633482). It offers some limited sport, but there are perhaps too many unclimbable waterfalls, so frequent diversions are needed into and out of the gorge. Due to the steep sides, these diversions aren't always trivial. Despite this, there are short steps of good scrambling, providing that some wading is undertaken, and the outlook towards the Yr Wyddfa (Snowdon) group is glorious. This is a very rich site for tiny liverworts;

boulder chokes hold toothed pouncewort (*Drepanolejeunea*) and pointed pouncewort (*Harpalejeunea*) as well as cowlwort (*Colura*). Occasional visits are unlikely to cause damage, but this is not an ideal site for large groups to walk up regularly. Just down from Gelli-Iago is another minor stream of interest, unnamed on maps, at SH 624466. This is on the heathery Yr Arddu to the west of Cnicht (there is another small hill of the same name to the north-east of Cnicht). The stream offers 70 m of extremely simple scrambling. It really isn't worth seeking out as a route, but for lovers of solitude it offers a pleasant way to the delightful Llyn yr Arddu. From here, the small hill of Yr Arddu can be roamed over, and its treasures discovered. Take a picnic; take some towels and have a swim (there are three lakes); scramble over the small outcrops; or take your climbing shoes and spend the day bouldering on the numerous boulders and craglets.

The gorge at Gelli Iago

Dyffryn Conwy (Conwy Valley) & Gwydyr Forest

Dyffryn Conwy is far removed from the central Snowdonia passes. Gone are the fearsome crags and mountain streams, replaced by fields, forests and the meandering Afon Conwy. Despite this, it makes a pleasant change from Dyffryn Ogwen and the Llanberis Pass. Cwm Eigiau facilitates a beautifully remote approach to the main Carneddau, whilst to the north Tal y Fan and friends can be accessed from Rowen. On the east side of the valley lies a hinterland of small hills and pretty valleys. Down towards Betws-y-Coed the Gwydyr Forest dominates an area scattered with lakes and abandoned mine workings, and explored primarily by mountain bikers. The valley rewards those who come looking for a new take on Snowdonia.

Within this area there are scrambles to be found, provided you know where to look. The wooded hillsides provide a picturesque backdrop to several gorge scrambles which can be used to spice up a day of meandering round the forest paths and tracks. This is a totally different game to scrambling on mountain buttresses and offers the chance for sport on a short afternoon, or perhaps when the main ranges are cloaked in mist.

There are campsites, bed and breakfasts and hotels scattered along the valley, with Betws-y-Coed being the popular tourist choice. This also makes travel east into the mountains simple.

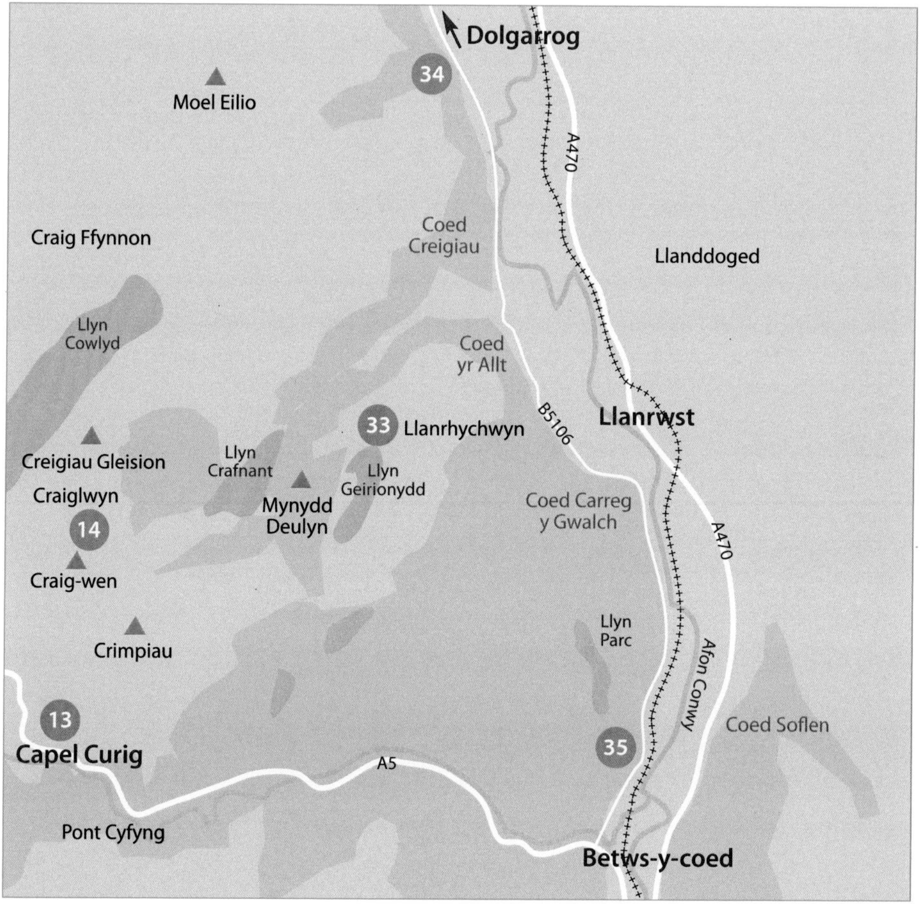
Dolgarrog
34
Moel Eilio
A470
Coed
Creigiau
Craig Ffynnon
Llanddoged
Llyn
Cowlyd
Coed
yr Allt
B5106
Llanrwst
33
Llanrhychwyn
Creigiau Gleision
Llyn
Crafnant
Llyn
Geirionydd
Craiglwyn
Mynydd
Deulyn
Coed Carreg
y Gwalch
14
A470
Craig-wen
Crimpiau
Llyn
Parc
Afon Conwy
13
Capel Curig
Coed Soflen
35
A5
Pont Cyfyng
Betws-y-coed

33. Geirionydd Gorge (1 or 2/3**)

In the hills to the south-west of Trefriw lies the picturesque Llyn Geirionydd, the second of Gwydyr's large lakes. The outflow at the northern end of the lake runs through a narrow gorge which gives a worthwhile scramble which can be combined with a spot of mine exploration. The abandoned Klondyke Lead Mine consists of numerous adits which the adventurous can explore. Immediately across the stream from the Klondyke Mill is a large, stone-lined entrance. This tunnel splits into three branches which eventually run out at dead ends (as of August 2009 these tunnels have been gated – now inaccessible and sadly gone the way of the majority of the Gwydyr mines). This adit was the site of the 'Klondyke Fraud' of 1918-1921. This involved one Joseph Aspinall coating the walls of the tunnel with lead concentrates to make them sparkle. He then claimed to have found a large deposit of silver, and employed large numbers of men to man the mining site. When Aspinall brought potential investors to the site the men would spring into action at the sound of his car, running around and generally looking productive. He thus managed to produce the appearance of a large silver mine, and managed to scam £166,000 before being found out and convicted. The book series "Mines of the

Gwydyr Forest" contain more information on Klondyke and the rest of the forest for those so inclined to such things. The rest of the gorge features more tunnels (most with large wooden supporting beams) but these are less stable and should not be investigated; there are vertical shafts about and accidents have occurred in the past. No name appears on OS maps for this gorge.

Meaning: The place belonging to Geirion.

Summary: Easy gorge scrambling with an optional hard technical start, and one unique and optional waterfall/tunnel pitch.

Conditions: The hard start is polished by water and therefore slippery. Higher up the rock is reasonably clean.

Height Gain: 100m

Approach: There is a car park near the south end of the lake. Walk north on the road alongside the lake. From the end of Llyn Geirionydd take a right of way that heads north on the east side of the gorge. As this drops down follow a path that forks off left and leads to the old Klondyke Mill (SH 765622).

Chris Peacock getting rinsed in the washing machine in the Geirionydd Gorge

Ascent: Despite their easy-angled appearance the opening slabs on the right-hand bank are technically quite hard (they earn their full grade only when wet), as well as being water-worn. Start along the slabs where a hard move comes immediately: using small hand holds you must lower/slide down to a foot ledge just above the water. A slip leads to a slide into deep water. Keep traversing along the water-side slabs using small ledges for feet. The handholds are generally quite small and the obvious traverse line gains height above the water making a slip less appealing. Continue along until the slabs run out. To avoid this hard start, take a path on the left-hand bank. Enter the bed and walk up the ravine where many tunnels begin to appear in the sides of the gorge.

Higher up the water cascades over a fall and enters a short tunnel, before re-emerging into the gorge. This is the ‘washing machine’ and offers a rather unique experience for the adventurous. Walk into the tunnel (with no choice but to get your feet wet) which brings you out below the waterfall. The exit doesn’t look easy, and it isn’t. The easiest option is to exit left in the corner (the water here is unexpectedly quite shallow thankfully). Make the most of good holds at the top, and use knees jammed against the rock, but be prepared to get a soaking from spray from the waterfall. This section can be avoided by easy scrambling up the dry streambed. Above this easy scrambling then walking leads back up to Llyn Geirionydd.

Usual Descents: N/A

Combinations: The gorge can be incorporated into a day exploring the various lakes and mines of the forest. Nearby Clogwyn Fuwch slate mine (SH 759618) is worth a visit and is found on the path from Geirionydd to Crafnant. A small tunnel beckons from the path which can be followed (take a torch) into a huge chamber, open to the light. Higher up the hill are more chambers and old buildings the curious can explore (though be extremely wary of hidden drops). The gorge could also be used as a prelude to a round of Creigiau Gleision via Crimpiau and Craig Wen (route 14). This would be done by taking one of the footpaths to Llyn Crafnant, then heading south-west and climbing up the path to the pass between Crimpiau and Clogwyn Manod

The starting slabs of the Geirionydd Gorge

34. Afon Ddu Gorge (2 or 3***) (V)

Hidden away on the wooded western slopes of Dyffryn Conwy above Dolgarrog two gorges cascade down from the fringes of the Carneddau. The Afon Ddu is the easier of the two; most of the scrambling is relatively simple (only the crux is worthy of a grade 3) and the quality of the rock ensures an enjoyable outing. Due to its roadside start it makes a pleasant evening's expedition. This would also go some way to avoiding the crowds from local outdoor centres that regularly use the gorge. Several notable bryophyte species occur including *Hygrohypnum duriusculum* and *Radula voluta*, but these are mostly on boulder sides/overhangs (perhaps because the river is already well-scrambled).

Meaning: Black river.

Summary: Good scrambling through scenic woodland with a technically hard but safe crux.

Conditions: The rock is mostly clean and sound, though some has been polished by the water.

Height Gain: 140m

Approach: From Pont Dolgarrog (where there is a parking area, SH 774663) enter the woods on a track (footpath sign), before turning left at the corner on a small path that leads down to the river. Besides the path is an information board on good practice.

Ascent: To begin with there are many possible ways to scramble up the gorge. Early on a rise is encountered with a small waterfall round to the left; here it is possible to scramble up the middle of the river bed, and crawl under the gap between two smooth boulders (getting wet in the process), then exiting upwards in a boulder choke.

The outlook changes when the walls steepen and the gorge narrows into a cleft, backed by waterfalls. If water levels are suitable it is often possible to wade this –

the water may come up to waist height if levels are low. Alternatively, a technical and delicate traverse can be attempted low along the right-hand wall. The third option is to leave the gorge before the pool using steps on the right.

A summer evening in the Afon Ddu Gorge

After the cleft, climb a short waterfall using a smooth scoop on the left. The waterfall above this is best avoided –

1. *Climbing the smooth scoop;*
2. *The huge unclimable fall in the Afon Ddu.*

instead turn ninety degrees right to cross the channel at the lip of the previous waterfall, and ascend a few metres up and out towards the right hand bank of the gorge. From here continue up as the gorge once more opens out offering a choice of line. Shortly you arrive at the base of a huge waterfall. Here look to the left bank where an easy escape (boulders, earth and moss) leads to steps and a path above the river bed. Follow these as they zig-zag up before allowing you to re-enter the bed above the big fall. From here more entertaining scrambling can be had. After a final few steps (best taken on the right) the angle of the river eases and a gate on the right gives access to a path leaving the gorge.

Usual Descents: Take the path into the woods past some water treatment works to reach a vehicle track. This leads steeply down to the road.

Combinations: A pathless ascent of the seldom-visited peak of Moel Eilio could be made from here, followed by a walk up Pen Llithrig y Wrach. Alternatively, the neglected summit of Creigiau Gleision could be climbed using tracks through the heather that wind up from the Llyn Cowlyd dam.

35. Aberllyn Gorge (1)

Llyn y Parc is an attractive lake in the Gwydyr Forest above Betws-y-Coed. Although natural, its water level was raised to drive turbines for the Aberllyn Mine (lead and zinc). From the lake's south end a stream departs and tumbles down the wooded slopes to enter the Afon Conwy, and this gorge makes a passable scramble. Most of the route is extremely easy grade 1, but the crux is quite tricky. Those with an interest in mining will enjoy the route as it passes through the site of the old mine.

Meaning: Mouth of the lake.

Summary: Mostly easy scrambling up a wooded gorge, with a tricky crux. Higher up the gorge can be escaped by moving left to a popular path.

Conditions: The rock is vegetation-free, but is incredibly smooth and slippery, especially on the crux.

Height Gain: 120m

Approach: Start in Betws-y-Coed at the car park and toilets over the bridge at SH 791567. Take the minor road east then turn right (north) after 150m on another small road. Follow the forestry track north-east as it rises then falls and passes a house called Greffyn. The track bends near a static caravan site and the stream is found under thick trees (SH 796577).

Ascent: Step over a wire fence to gain the gloomy stream. Walk up the stony bed passing a crescent-shaped opening in the right bank. At first the scrambling is easy, and various mining artefacts appear (old bricks, tanks, concrete sandbags). Interest increases as the stream flows down a narrow culverted channel. Climb up over assorted logs and the stream turns right. This is the crux.

Climb the first step easily. The next small fall is deceptively tricky, as well as being incredibly smooth. It is best taken on the left. There is no exposure but a slip could still break an ankle. The footholds are uncomfortably small and so the best solution is to pull up on two good water-worn pockets high up, whilst jamming knees against the rock. Above this, mantelshelf a final step to regain easy ground.

The gorge opens out here and the scrambling is bouldery and easy. A gated brick-lined adit is seen on the left with water flowing out of it; this is the stream water. Consequently, the gorge above this point is completely dry. Climb two boulder blockages and water reappears in the bed. More concrete sandbags are passed and another short steepening provides more interest. The route finishes up rocks below a waterfall by mine buildings. Leave the stream on the left below this fall to gain the path.

Usual Descents: Follow the right of way beside the gorge back down towards Betws-y-Coed.

Combinations: Follow the path north to Llyn y Parc. Numerous walks can be fashioned through the forest, simply following paths and tracks to various old mines and lakes. For those wanting another scrambling fix, the Geirionydd Gorge (route 33) is approximately four miles away.

One of the boulder blockages in the Aberllyn Gorge

Dyffryn Conwy & Gwydyr Forest – Further Scrambling Opportunities

There are scant other scrambling opportunities in this area that can be recommended. Just north of the Afon Ddu is the gorge of the Afon Porth Llwyd (also known as Dolgarrog Gorge, although confusingly some refer to the Afon Ddu as Dolgarrog Gorge) (SH 767676). This does get used by outdoor groups, but cannot be recommended in this text. This is because the river can flash flood due to water release from upstream at the Coedty Reservoir; something to do with a tipper (or two tippers) that controls water flow. My information is lacking in detail. Either way, the gorge is probably best left alone. Additionally, the ravine holds several large boulders on which tiny, scarce liverworts grow. The upper wooded slopes are even richer, with the rare Atlantic featherwort as well as copious mosses and liverworts. Further north along the valley again is the Afon Dulyn (SH 764687). This certainly has one waterfall on it and looks promising, though I have never been for a closer look. Bouldery sections of the river generate mist that supports a rich array of liverworts, and the raspberry-like stone bramble sprawls across the ravine side in one area.

Rhaeadr Ewynnol (meaning "foaming" but mistranslated to Swallow Falls) looks to give brief and interesting scrambling but is a highly sensitive SSSI with *Schistidium agassizii* on rocks on the river margin and a diverse range of liverworts. Gorge scramblers should therefore refrain from exploring the falls.

There are two interesting looking streams on the west side of Llyn Crafnant. I have explored the Afon Hendre at SH 738606 behind Hendre. Many people passing this way will be aware of the stream as there is a scenic waterfall adjacent to the path. This fall can be climbed by a groove on the far left (note the old ceramic tank in the stream at the top) but beyond this the stream disappoints. At first there is some pleasant scrambling and wading, but higher up the pools become too deep and progress must be made on the banks. This is painful going; all spindly trees and bramble bashing. After what feels like an eternity of fighting the jungle the ford is reached at SH 738608 and the right of way can be followed once more. It is possible that the stream above the ford may offer better scrambling (indeed, another fall can be seen in the trees) but it has not been investigated. On the same side of the lake is the Ceunant y Parc (SH 745609) which might be worth a closer look.

Heading out from Dyffryn Conwy onto the mountains, Craig Eigiau might offer some sport. Both the stream at SH 716650 and the buttresses to the south (especially those above Cedryn at SH 718639 which are more broken in nature) might prove fruitful. The upper reaches off the Afon Eigiau also look delightful; a mix of deep pools and scrambling opportunities. The brave might be tempted to delve into the dark heart of Foel Grach and explore the rakes and gullies of Craig y Dulyn (SH 697664). This is serious ground. Upwards we go, to the tiny lake of Ffynnon Llyffant (SH 688646), nestling below the summit of Carnedd Llewelyn. From the south end of the lake, a broad and rocky low-relief ridge runs up to arrive just east of the summit and offers some scrambling. This is a long way to come to find some rocky sport, but the solitude more than compensates.

There is one final gorge in the area to mention, and that is the Afon Conwy at Ffos Noddum (Fairy Glen) just south of Betws-y-Coed. It's a popular tourist spot, and entrance to the grounds of Fairy Glen is just off the A470 (SH 798546) and is signed. Payment is via an honesty box, and a path runs above the gorge before descending to the riverside. From the head of the gorge the nature of the place can be appraised; deep black pools, beetling walls. A traverse of the gorge from here to Rhaeadr y Graig Lwyd (Conwy Falls) is possible, but really falls outside the scope of this book. It is true canyoning, not scrambling, and involves swimming as well as scrambling. Indeed, your humble author nearly drowned on one swimming passage in the gorge and was rescued by a friend (thanks Mark!). The passage is just under a mile in length, yet took us (as a party of four) four and a half hours, and that involved leaving the gorge to avoid certain obstacles and pools. Needless to say that going into the gorge in anything other than prolonged drought conditions would be foolhardy. I cannot recommend it at all. The deep ravine holds plenty of populations of the exceedingly small long-leaved pouncewort (*Aphanolejeunea microscopica*), whilst pinnate scalewort (*Porella pinnata*) grows submerged in the river. There are rare lichens here too, growing where the river inundates them from time to time, including several species of *Dermatocarpon* and *Sticta*. There may be friendlier scrambling further along the Afon Conwy from Pont Padog (SH 839514), but we are now into the realm of pure speculation.

1. Scrambling above deep water in Fairy Glen; 2 Dave Jackon surveying the way ahead in Fairy Glen.

2

North Wales Coast

For those heading to mountain adventures the north Wales coast is generally seen as a picturesque blur beside the A55. Pretty enough, but incomparable to the Snowdonian highlands. Fair enough; the coastal area cannot match the grandeur of the mountains, but it does repay the occasional away day with its pleasant mix of woodlands, moorland and hillside. On a sunny day the attraction is increased, with the glittering sea stretching away, dotted with tankers and wind turbines.

To convince the stubborn, there is one excellent scramble to add some excitement to an exploratory wander. There are numerous towns along the coast (Bangor, Llanfairfechan, Penmaenmawr and Conwy) where a base could be made, all linked by a good bus and rail service, thus offering potential for linear days.

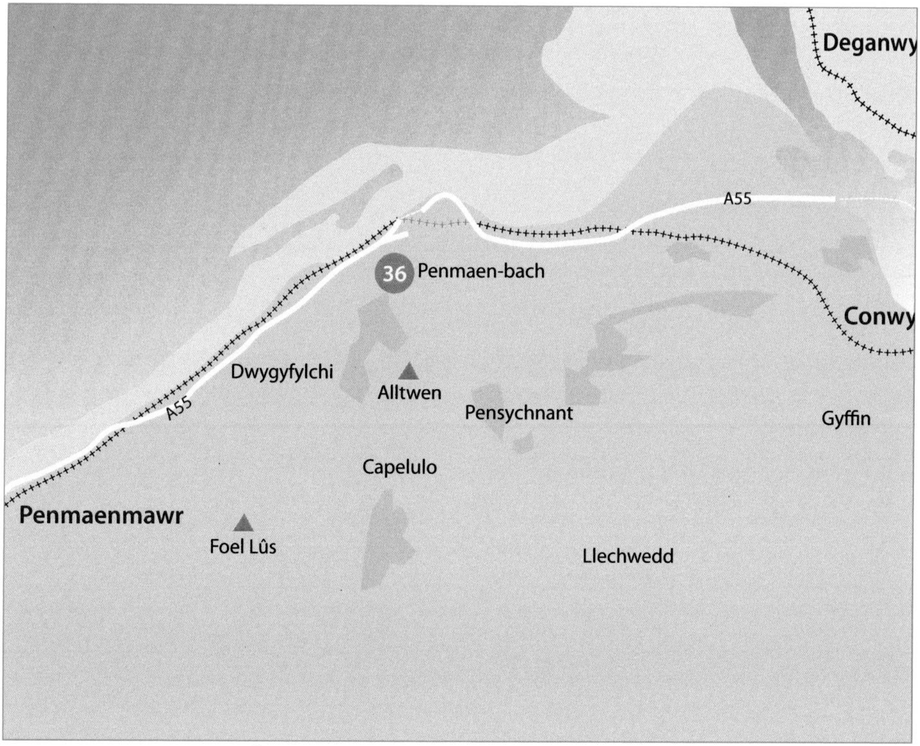
Deganwy
A55
36 Penmaen-bach
Conwy
Dwygyfylchi
Alltwen
A55
Pensychnant
Gyffin
Capelulo
Penmaenmawr
Foel Lûs
Llechwedd

36. Penmaen Bach Arête (2**)

Driving along the A55 from Penmaenmawr to Conwy, and just before entering the road tunnel, a striking arête is seen off to the right. Surely this compelling line must call out to all passing scramblers? Yet, in all my journeys past I have never observed a single person on the ridge. This is the Penmaen Bach Arête; an airy and exciting short scramble. Use it as an excuse to explore the hills, paths and ancient monuments of the coastal zone.

Meaning: Lesser stone headland.

Summary: Airy scrambling up a narrow roadside arête.

Conditions: There is some loose rock and the route would potentially be very slippery in the wet.

Height Gain: 125m

Approach: The route starts at SH 743781. A direct approach could be made through the caravan site at Pendyffryn Hall, although this might not go down too well with the owners. The cautious can park on the road at the bottom of Bwlch Sychnant (Sychnant Pass) and take the footpath at SH 742769 that heads north. When it bears right uphill, keep ahead on access land to arrive at the base of the obvious arête.

Ascent: The start is obvious. Climb upwards taking care with any gorse bushes that may be encountered. The major distraction is noise from the A55 below, but scramblers on the ridge are probably distracting to drivers too! Most of the scrambling is simple, but there are several harder steps where some thought is required. After a short while the arête merges with the slopes of Penmaen Bach. A descent can be made from here down unstable scree slopes (left of the arête, facing out) but by continuing up some grade 1 scrambling can be had until scree takes over to the 245m summit which offers excellent views along the coast.

Scenic views over the North Wales Expressway on Penmaen Bach Arête

Usual Descents: By heading south towards Alltwen the right of way can be followed back to the bottom of Bwlch Sychnant.

Combinations: Those who want to spend the rest of the day exploring are spoilt for choice. Mynydd y Dref (Conwy Mountain) and Alltwen can both by taken in using a network of paths, before heading to the pretty Bwlch Sychnant. From here the moors below Tal y Fan are littered with stone circles, hut circles and various old ruins which will be of interest to some. Tal y Fan itself is also a worthy target that offers good views of Dyffryn Conwy and the high Carneddau on a clear day.

North Wales Coast – Further Scrambling Opportunities

Unfortunately, the above route is pretty much all that the area has to offer. There are other scree shoots and buttresses on Penmaen Bach, but they are best left alone; explorers run the all-too-real risk of dislodging large quantities of loose rock down on to the A55. Further along the coast is Mynydd y Dref (Conwy Mountain). On the east ridge there is a short, steep slab (SH 766778). It certainly isn't worth seeking out, but if you're walking in the area it offers about five minutes of scrambling and climbing entertainment. Similarly, above Llanfairfechan at SH 689733 is the small rock outcrop of Garreg Fawr, identified by the stone walls below it. The outcrop offers a range of lines and provides a modicum of scrambling if passing. It could be visited on an approach to the shapely and ignored ridge that runs above Cwm Anafon from Foel Dduarth to Drum.

Hiding in the woods behind Capelulo is another Fairy Glen (SH 744761). This used to be a popular tourist attraction but is now private, and the old paths are considerably overgrown. There is access land at the base of the stream, but none higher up. Curiously there is a fragment of right of way further up, but it connects with nothing else. There are numerous small waterfalls in the stream, but it cannot be recommended due to the access difficulties.

Heading into the mountains now, determined scramblers could seek out some rock on the north spur of Bera Mawr in the Carneddau. Beyond Rhaeadr Fawr (Aber Falls) the lonely valley of the Afon Goch stretches into the heart of Carneddau. This valley is entered by taking a rising path across scree on the east side of the waterfall (there are some wet rock shelves at the top which sometimes catch out the unwary). From here, Bera Mawr draws the eye with its northern ramparts of craglets. It's a long walk in for little reward, but a contrived scramble can be made up the northern spur (SH 674687) linking boulder fields and rock steps to the summit tor. More micro-scrambles can then be had to gain the adjacent summit of Bera Bach. In the same area, I have often pondered a gully on Marian Rhaeadr Fawr, the cliff to the east of Rhaeadr Fawr (Aber Falls). This gully is passed on the aforementioned rising scree path, and is known as Aber Gully, grade I/II, in the winter climbing guide. I wonder if a summer ascent is feasible?

On Anglesey there is plenty of rock on Mynydd Tŵr (Holyhead mountain), and some scrambling can be found on the south-east "ridge", starting from around SH 219826. On Pen Llŷn (Llŷn Peninsula) there are a few possibilities situated around the hill of Yr Eifl. Firstly, there are a handful of small buttresses (e.g. SH 375444) scattered across the slopes of Tre'r Ceiri; the determined might find some micro-scrambles here. Secondly, the large boulder field (SH 367448) encountered when ascending Yr Eifl from Tre'r Ceiri offers a brief clamber. Finally, there is a 444m outlier of Yr Eifl that is nameless on OS maps, but is known as Garn For (SH 361457). Steep cliffs drop down to the sea from its summit. I have not personally explored the cliffs, but the 1955 Climbers' Club journal references various routes here: Diagonal Gully (a scramble), Wrong Rib (graded mod, "occasional scrambling pitches are separated by long walks"), Pinnacle Gully and Central Gully (both "walking only"), Stoneshoot Gully (described as "unpleasant scrambling up gravel and loose rocks"). At the far south end of the cliff is the headland of Trwyn y Gorlech, which presents an arresting profile when viewed from Porth y Nant. An intrepid scrambler might have a fruitful day exploring these cliffs, or might come home empty handed.

Eifionydd

The Eifionydd mountains see few visiting walkers and climbers when compared to neighbouring ranges. The pull of Yr Wyddfa from across Nant y Betws is enough to draw many elsewhere. Despite this the area is excellent walking territory. A trek along the Nantlle Ridge, spiced with small sections of scrambling makes a memorable day, as does a traverse of the three moels: Moel Lefn, Moel yr Ogof and Moel Hebog. The region also hosts some excellent climbers' crags, such as the slabby Craig yr Ogof or the imposing Castell Cidwm.

Unfortunately, the scrambler does not have such joys. A handful of routes were described in Scrambles in Snowdonia, with the crumbling Sentries Ridge on Mynydd Mawr being the pick of the bunch. There are alternative entertainments to be had, however, for those willing to explore. The Afon Goch is particularly worthwhile, due to its stunning situation below an ignored cwm.

A base in Beddgelert is the most pleasing, but Caernarfon is equally convenient. For those wanting to camp there are sites at Betws Garmon and the Beddgelert forest. There is also bed and breakfast accommodation at Rhyd Ddu.
An aside: not all of the following routes fall within the commote of Eifionydd. I am, however, following the example of Steve Ashton's "Scrambles in Snowdonia" which used the same name for the range.

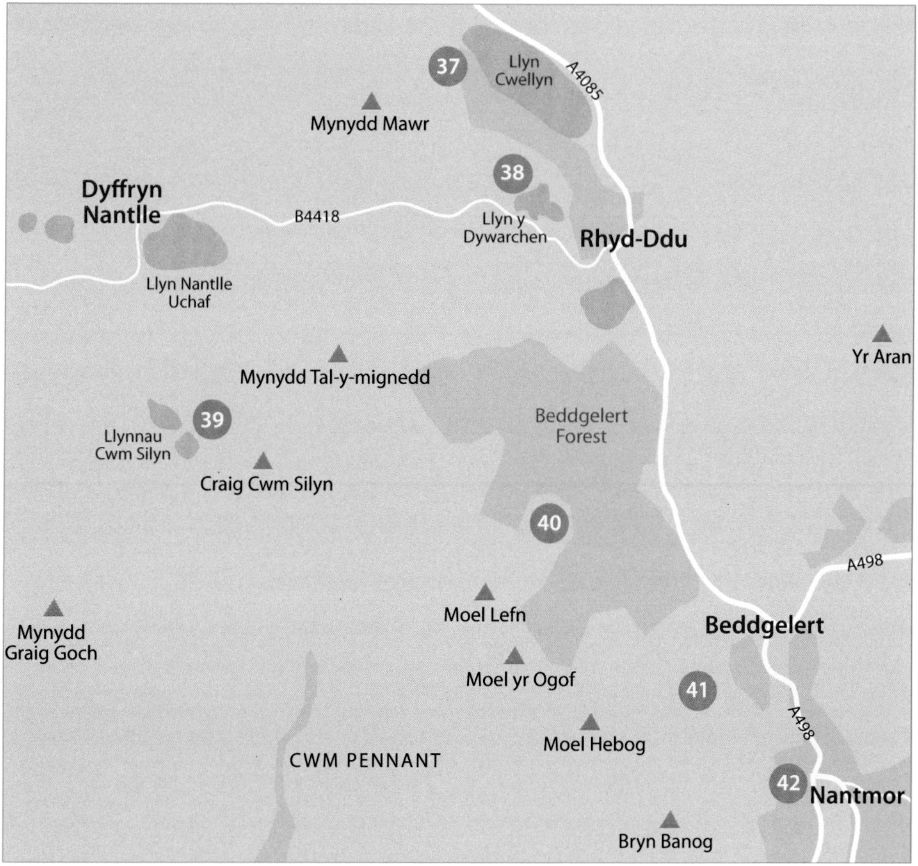
37
Llyn Cwellyn
A4085
Mynydd Mawr
38
Dyffryn Nantlle
B4418
Llyn y Dywarchen
Rhyd-Ddu
Llyn Nantlle Uchaf
Yr Aran
Mynydd Tal-y-mignedd
Beddgelert Forest
39
Llynnau Cwm Silyn
Craig Cwm Silyn
40
A498
Moel Lefn
Beddgelert
Mynydd Graig Goch
Moel yr Ogof
41
A498
Moel Hebog
CWM PENNANT
42
Nantmor
Bryn Banog

37. Afon Goch (Llyn Cwellyn) (1/2**)

Mynydd Mawr sits alone across Llyn Cwellyn and thus makes a fine viewpoint for the surrounding area. Most people climb it using a path on the north-west ridge, or from Rhyd Ddu via Foel Rudd. East of the summit the slopes drop down into empty Cwm Planwydd, which is drained by the Afon Goch. Although open in nature, the stream provides some excellent scrambling and certainly deserves a visit. The views back over Llyn Cwellyn to Yr Wyddfa are excellent.

Meaning: Red river.

Summary: Good scrambling in a beautiful location.

Conditions: Some rock is slimy but the holds are good on the crux sequence.

Height Gain: 150m

Approach: There is a large car park in Rhyd Ddu. Walk up the road past the Cwellyn Arms and turn left onto the Nantlle road. Pass a row of houses and a side street, then turn right onto a forest track. Head north-west, using forest tracks beside Llyn Cwellyn, to leave the forest and arrive below the fearsome crag of Castell Cidwm (SH 551554). Cross the stream and climb a wall, and head left around some trees. Gain the stream wherever feasible. An approach could be made from Planwydd (SH 568539) if using the bus, but signs prohibit parking here. There is no access land at the north-west end of the lake, thus removing the possibility of a short approach there.

Ascent: Simple walking/scrambling soon brings you to the crux waterfall. One steep fall comes in from the left, whilst the main (right) branch flows down a series of little steps. This is the crux and once committed is not escapable. Never fear however, for it presents few problems. Climb up, generally sticking to the right, and using good holds.

Now the landscape opens out, and escape is always possible. Scramble up, enjoying some clean and sound rock on the right side of the watercourse. Further up one small fall cannot be climbed directly. Masochists of slime can choose to ascend to the left, others may decide to walk around. From here it is a simple matter of upwards progress, making the most of any dry rock that is stream-side. Another fall higher up must also be avoided. Eventually the gradient relents leaving you in Cwm Planwydd.

Usual Descents: A direct descent can be made using a track on the left side of the stream (looking down) to return you to the lake.

Combinations: A favourable plan is to head up the grassy northern spur of Foel Rudd. You can then proceed to the summit of Mynydd Mawr, or descend to Rhyd Ddu for a well-earned pint. Do not attempt (as I once did) a direct route to the summit cairn on Craig Cwm Bychan; this is a purgatory of deep heather and muscle-burning steepness (though there is some aircraft wreckage strewn in a scree gully that might be of interest to some).

Adam Pearce and Si Oakley above Llyn Cwellyn on the Afon Goch

38. Clogwyn y Garreg (1*)

Clogwyn y Garreg is a modest lump of some 336m height. From most viewpoints it appears insignificant, but when driving east along Dyffryn Nantlle it commands the head of the valley, and sports a couple of enticing rocky ribs. The described route is just one possibility, and gives an excuse to take in the summit view, which must be one of the best in Snowdonia when considering the effort:view ratio. Llyn y Dywarchen is directly below, then comes Llyn y Gader. In the distance the northern Rhinogau can be glimpsed, with Foel Penolau showing its distinctive square-cut profile. Closer to home are Yr Wyddfa (Snowdon) and Yr Aran, plus an unusual view of the chossy cliffs of Y Garn, whilst behind is Mynydd Mawr and the loose crag of Craig y Bera.

Meaning: Stoney crags.

Summary: A short scramble up a rocky rib to a minor summit.

Conditions: The rock quality is good.

Height Gain: 80m

Approach: There is a car park (used by fishermen) with space for a few vehicles at SH 559533. Take the path along the west shore of Llyn y Dywarchen and cross a stile. From here head left up boggy ground in the little bwlch between Clogwyn y Garreg on the right, and Bryn Gwyn on the left. Descend a little to what is presumably an old mining track which heads right (north). This leads under a mini-buttress flecked with quartz – the start of the scramble.

Ascent: Climb the buttress on its left side. Above, the main sweep of the rib can be surveyed; its right edge forms a considerable cliff, and the base of the rib terminates in a stone wall. Head up to the base, which necessitates a few unpleasant moments on grass, and carefully cross the wall. From here the scrambling consists of short, technical slabs (which can be made harder or easier) to the summit. If the right edge is followed then the exposure is quite serious.

Usual Descents: Head east off the summit, with a short down-scramble off the top rocks. Grassy slopes can then be followed back to the shore of Llyn y Dywarchen. The lake used to be notable for containing a small floating island which was present as late as 1931. Geraint Roberts ("The Lakes of Eryri") suggests the island was a section of peaty bank that was kept floating due to methane produced by decaying plants. There used to be a second lake (Llyn Bwlch y Moch – its dam is still visible) on the other side of Clogwyn y Garreg which also had an odd phenomenon. According to Frank Ward ("The Lakes of Wales") a small island rose above the water in summer, and fell during winter. Like the floating island, the proffered explanation is that it was caused by gas.

Combinations: Scramblers can head a short distance to a path that leads through the forest to the Afon Goch (route 37), or make a beeline to Sentries Ridge on Craig y Bera. Those just after a walk can ascend Mynydd Mawr via Foel Rudd.

1. Rachel Harvey on the quartz-flecked buttress at the start of the Clogwyn y Garreg scramble; 2. The scramble may be short but the summit view makes it worthwhile.

39. The Great Stone Shoot of Cwm Silyn (1*)

Cwm Silyn is one of the great cwms of Eryri. Twin lakes sit below a cirque of tremendous crags; on the left are the rocky prows of Craig Fawr and Craig yr Ogof, followed by chossy ground around Four Pitch Gully and then the impressive amphitheatre of the Little Kitchen. Finally, the deep, forked gash of Bedrock Gully cleaves Clogwyn y Cysgod. Despite this, few people visit, for this is surely the realm of the climber? Ignore first impressions, for the Great Stone Shoot allows a close-up look at the tilting precipices with little difficulty.

Summary: Bouldery walking and scrambling up a mountain gully, followed by a finish on scree.

Conditions: Loose rock and scree abound, and a helmet is advised.

Height Gain: 120m

Approach: The best starting point is the end of the narrow road at Maen-llwyd (SH 495511) above Llanllyfni (near Penygroes). Cars can be parked in a field beyond a gate at the roadhead. From here, a track leads across the moor to the cwm. Other, more taxing approaches can be made from the Nantlle Valley.

The route can be spied in advance from across the lakes. Craig yr Ogof is the steep nose above the right end of the lake. It has a triangular front and a slabby right wall. To the right of this is Amphitheatre Gully, and right again is the Great Stone Shoot. Follow the path past the lakes, and slog up on paths through bilberries and scree until level with the base of the crag. This wall is the most popular with climbers. The Great Stone Shoot is ahead, running up to a low point on the skyline.

Ascent: The usual climbing descent route take ground to the right of the Great Stone Shoot (looking up) but an ascent of the Shoot provides more interest. Enter the bouldery gully, amid impressive rock scenery. The route is mainly walking until a fork is reached. The left branch has a slimy pitch, so take the right branch where the first real bit of proper scrambling is

1. Imposing rock architecture, and views back to Llynnau Cwm Silyn; 2. The fork in the gully; 3. Low down in the Great Stone Shoot of Cwm Silyn.

called for. Above this are short, mossy steps. Dispatch some of these, then move left where feasible out of the gully. This brings about a position on the crest between the two branches of the gully. Upwards progress is then made over grass and rock, until a final stretch of steep scree gains the top by a central tower of rock and a fence and wall. The summit is a short walk away to the east.

Usual Descents: The rim of Cwm Silyn can be followed over Clogwyn y Cysgod and back to the car.

Combinations: One pleasant option is to head south-west to Garnedd Goch, then down to the top of Mynydd Graig Goch. Slopes of heather, bilberries and grass lead north-west down to the head of Llyn Cwm Dulyn, then access land or rights of way can be used to regain the start.

40. Castell to Moel Lefn Traverse (1*)

Moel Lefn is often climbed as either the first or last hill in a traverse of itself, Moel yr Ogof and Moel Hebog. Indeed, it is a popular route with hillwalkers. Below it to the north-east lies Castell, a rocky and wild summit rising out of Beddgelert Forest, and by visiting this top first an unusual approach can be made to Moel Lefn. Even better is the fact that numerous small scrambling opportunities can be had on both peaks.

Meaning: Castle.

Summary: Optional scrambling on outcrops over an unfrequented minor peak, followed by an ascent of Moel Lefn using a scree gully and further outcrops.

Conditions: The rock quality is excellent, and vegetation absent.

Height Gain: 150m on Castell, 140m on Moel Lefn (both include some walking)

Approach: The best start point is the Pont Cae'r Gors Forestry Commission car park (SH 573502). Numerous approaches are feasible. One pleasant option is to visit Llyn Llywelyn first. In this case, take the new path leading out of the north side of the car park. This crosses the Welsh Highland Railway at a level crossing and leads to a forestry track. Turn left along this and follow it (ignoring two possible right hand turns) until a track leads up to the lake. It is a beautiful spot, and on a hot day the temptation is to linger here.

To reach the scramble retrace your steps to the crossroads at SH 566501 and turn right. Another track on the right (by a scenically-positioned bench) winds up to the base of Castell. On some maps a footpath is marked from Llyn Llywelyn towards this spot, but the path can no longer be found in the undergrowth. At around about SH 565495 quit the track and gain the eastern slopes of Castell (unfortunately this involves negotiating a barbed-wire fence).

Ascent: The terrain on the forest edge is bracken, with heather and gorse springing up. Various little rock outcrops can be

spied. Proceed upwards, heading towards any fun-looking micro-scrambles. One particular pleasant section is found on the right of the slopes: a mini crag is split by a heathery recess, and the left-hand rib is very enjoyable. From here heathery walking is interspersed with optional rock steps to the first false summit (388m). More walking and scrambling then brings about a second false summit (approx 430m). A stone's throw from here is the real top (approx 440m), gained by descending a few metres then clambering up a few steps (the right-slanting break in one makes a very satisfying micro-scramble). The views of Beddgelert Forest,

1. Adam Pearce on the mini crag near the start; 2. Ascending the gully on Moel Lefn.

the Nantlle Ridge and Yr Wyddfa are all excellent.

From the summit of Castell, a careful descent round rock steps leads to a flat area. Beyond this lies a small buttress of volcanic rock columns which makes another interesting scramble. Proceed south-west towards Moel Lefn following traces of a path, and crossing a dry stone wall. The slopes of Moel Lefn are bounded on the right by rocks. In the centre is a steep grassy slope, and to the left is a broken buttress. This buttress is the target.

Once closer it becomes apparent that the right hand rocks of the buttress are chossy and unpleasant. Ignore them, and climb left across scree. Beyond a more sustained crag a scree gully issues from above. Either go up the gully (noting more rock columns on the right) which has one steeper step, or move out left onto heathery ground. Above, the slopes open out and various scrambling sections can be had on excellent rock. One final photogenic finish is to move left and ascend a low-gradient rib. Suddenly, the ground relents and the summit appears a short walk away across grass.

Usual Descents: By following the path north to Bwlch Cwm Trwsgl a right of way can be joined leading back into Beddgelert Forest.

Combinations: Moel yr Ogof is the next summit to the south and is an easy walk. Beyond that Moel Hebog can be ascended rather steeply, followed by a descent towards Beddgelert. Glyndwr's Cave is also worth a visit. This lies on the eastern cliffs of Moel yr Ogof and is best found from above. Just before Bwlch Meillionen is reached on descent from Moel yr Ogof faint paths lead left through a landscape of humps and hollows. Careful probing eventually leads to a spot above a large grassy gully. At the back of the gully lies a cleft, but this is not the cave in question. In fact, it is an asbestos mine. From the mine precarious ledges lead above the

gully and onto the face of the buttress where the exposure increases and the cave is found. Not for the faint-hearted, and not for me either; I've never made it beyond the mine. On returning to Bwlch Meillionen, a path leads into the forest where a way can be contrived back to the start.

1. Lovely views over Llyn Llywelyn; 2. Adrian Luescher maximising the scrambling opportunities; 3. The photogenic finale of the Castell to Moel Lefn Traverse.

41. Nant Cwmcloch (1*)

Moel Hebog stands sentinel over the south-western end of Nant Gwynant. From the tourist-thronged streets of Beddgelert, I always feel that it looks taller than its modest height of 782 m. It is commonly climbed as either the first or last peak in a traverse including its neighbours Moel yr Ogof and Moel Lefn. The tourist path ascends the spur between Cwm Llwy and Cwm Bleiddiaid (probably best ignore that right of way that seemingly levitates up the cliff on the OS map), but the Y Diffwys ridge also offers a quieter route to the summit. However, around the corner the Nant Cwmcloch is found; an open streamway that gently climbs the lower flanks of the hill. For scramblers it offers an easy but pleasant way of gaining height.

Meaning: Stream of the cwm of the bell.

Summary: Easy and open scrambling up a gentle stream.

Conditions: The rock quality is good. Probably best enjoyed on a dry day in low flow to get the most out of the scrambling.

Height Gain: 200m

Approach: From the car park in Beddgelert (SH 587481) follow a path (that stays on the north side of the railway) that runs north-west. This goes under the railway to meet a minor road. Turn left and follow the road upwards past a few houses and over two level crossings. The tourist trail for Moel Hebog leaves the track at SH 581479, but ignore this and follow the right of way south-east past another house. Just before Bron Hebog is reached, turn right to pick up a right of way (no obvious path) that climbs a very boggy field. This crosses a disused leat (look out for the rusting remains of some associated metalwork) to reach the top of the field. From here a new gate off to the right leads into another rough field which can be crossed to reach the stream. However, it should be noted that this is not access land. To keep to access land you have to climb upwards

1. *A view to the easy-angled Nant Cwmcloch;*
2. *Easy and escapable, but enjoyable, scrambling.*

(south) for 400 m (distance, not height gain) beside the plantation, before then traversing across to the Nant Cwmcloch and descending to the start of the scrambling. It would also be feasible to reach the Nant Cwmcloch lower down at SH 580476, by taking the aforementioned Moel Hebog path and abandoning it for a pathless approach on access land, which is more plentiful on the western side of the stream.

Easy scrambling besides the bluebells

Ascent: From below, the stream is seen to steadily rise, with hints of small cascades in its upper reaches. Lower down are numerous traverses and short steps, all very easy, and best enjoyed by wading up the stream. The outlook behind, of the Yr Wyddfa group, Cnicht, and a distant Moel Siabod, improves as height is won. Higher up the bouldery nature of the stream changes as rock slabs and steps appear, and some very deep pools are found. One notable obstacle is a steeper waterfall which can be taken easily on the far left, or with more difficulty (grade 2) on the right. More scrambling leads up to where a wall comes down to the stream. Beyond this the scrambling soon peters out.

Usual Descents: It would be possible to simply walk down beside the stream, and then exit in the same manner as the approach.

Combinations: From the top of the stream the eastern summit cliffs of Moel Hebog present a fearsome sight. They are cleaved by the gully of Glyndŵr's Ladder which was given a climbing grade of 'easy' in the Climbers' Club Cwm Silyn and Cwellyn guidebook. This is an old grade, seldom used these days and suggests that the route falls within the territory of a scramble, but I have never ascended the gully and so cannot offer any robust advice. To reach the summit of Moel Hebog by more conventional means, trend north-west to pick up the main path. It is also possible to head south and slog up the south-eastern shoulder of the mountain, but this is extremely steep in places, and something of a grind. From Moel Hebog a descent is best made to Bwlch Meillionen where one option is to follow the path down into Beddgelert Forest and homewards. Mountaineers will scorn this early descent to the pub, and continue the walk over Moel yr Ogof and Moel Lefn. From Bwlch Cwm-trwsgl a path can be followed that leads pleasantly through the forest and across the slopes of Castell. Once in the forest numerous ways lead home, but the simplest is to locate the new bridleway that runs between Rhyd-Ddu and Beddgelert.

For those who have no interest in visiting the summit of Moel Hebog, it is possible to free-range over to Bryn Bannog and then onto the outlying top of Moel Ddu, perhaps with a return down towards Nantmor and along the Pass of Aberglaslyn.

42. Afon Goch (Nantmor) (1)

Pont Aberglaslyn lies at the southern end of its namesake pass. Beyond here the Afon Glaslyn, that started life high on Yr Wyddfa, makes a final leisurely course for the sea. The Afon Goch is hidden in the trees near Pont Aberglaslyn, and offers an easy and accessible scramble through scenic woodland.

Meaning: Red river.

Summary: Easy and escapable scrambling up a woodland stream.

Conditions: Moss is present on some of the steps.

Height Gain: 100m

Approach: The easiest starting point is the small pay and display car park in Nantmor at SH 597462. Either walk along the road, or take the path through the woods, to reach Pont Aberglaslyn. For the longer but more dramatic approach, start in Beddgelert and take the path down the Pass of Aberglaslyn (on the east side of the river) to reach the same bridge. From Pont Aberglaslyn, walk south down the road for about 100 m. Just before Aberglaslyn Hall, a footpath leaves the road (SH 594461) on the right. This goes behind the hall to a footbridge on the Afon Goch.

Ascent: Follow the stream upwards over boulders and rocks. Several mossy cascades provide sport, with the most enjoyment generally to be had by following the water. At one point an old track ends at the stream, perhaps suggesting that a bridge used to exist here. Higher up, the gradient eases at a water tank and pipe before another minor cascade is reached. Easy scrambling leads past a wooden structure on the left bank that appears to be a sheltered sleeping platform, presumably used by local outward bound groups. Further up a fence is reached. Step over this, and the stream narrows to give a few more scrambly steps before vegetation encroaches and the angle eases. Escape to the left through the undergrowth to find a footpath beside the stream.

Usual Descents: The path leads back down to the starting point. Numerous trees beside the path have reflectors attached; presumably to help find the sleeping shelter in the dark.

Combinations: Keen scramblers could tramp over to the Nant Cwmcloch (route 41), about a mile away. Alternatively, the summit of Moel Ddu is within easy reach. The remains of the small hillfort of Pen y Gaer (SH 586457) are a few hundred metres from the top of the stream for those interested in such things.

Gareth Harvey and Tom Hecht on the Afon Goch (Nantmor)

Eifionydd – Further Scrambling Opportunities

Glyndŵr's Ladder has already been mentioned under the Nant Cwmcloch. This is a gully which is graded as 'easy' in the Climbers' Club Cwm Silyn and Cwellyn guidebook. This is an old grade, suggesting an easy rock climb, but I have not investigated further. On the Diffwys face of Moel Hebog is a rake called The Companionway. It is graded I as a winter climb and I have heard that it offers an unusual scramble that slants upwards across the face from left to right (looking up to Moel Hebog's summit). Like Glyndŵr's Ladder I have never been for a closer look, alas.

On the unpopular side of Moel Hebog is Cwm Pennant. This long valley burrows into the heart of the mountains, but is generally quiet, with few walkers visiting it. At the northern end of the valley is the Ceunant yr Allt (SH 539500). It is possible to ascend this ravine (grade 1). The scrambling is poor, but the outlook and atmosphere are excellent. From the top of the ravine it is possible to ascend to either Bwlch Dros-bern, or to slog up the south-eastern ridge of Mynydd Tal y Mignedd. Elsewhere in Cwm Pennant, there are twin streams on access land above Braichydinas at SH 530484 and 531484 that look promising.

Near Rhyd-Ddu is an interesting little stream on Y Garn that drains Cwm Marchnad. The path to Cwm Pennant crosses it at SH 558517. It is narrow, and flows between slopes of grass and gorse, and always looks worthy of a visit.

Early editions of Scrambles in Snowdonia make a passing mention to Central Rake in Craig Cwm Du on Mynydd Mawr. This is apparently grade 2 with a hard start.

Heading south almost to Porthmadog is Moel Ddu, an outlier of Moel Hebog. There is some rock here, and I have long pondered a scrambling ascent from just above Gelli-lydan up the south-east shoulder probably starting from SH 586434.

A view of Glyndŵr's Ladder

The Vale of Ffestiniog and the Moelwynion

The Vale of Ffestiniog is a lengthy valley that runs from Blaenau Ffestiniog south, then west towards Porthmadog. It is bounded first by the Moelwynion and the Ffestiniog Hills. The former are one of the criminally ignored ranges of north Wales; a vast, sprawling array of hills and mountains, offering both airy summits and boggy plateaus. The latter are even more neglected, and, in the case of one mountain, unnamed by the OS. The North Top of Manod Mawr (a Hewitt and Nuttall) is a melancholy place, almost devoured as it is by the adjacent quarry. Blaenau itself can be a dark place of grey houses and grey towers of slate waste, yet when the sun shines over Tanygrisiau Reservoir there is a certain beauty to the area. The mines and quarries certainly add an extra point of interest to the area, whether your predilection is for poking around at surface artefacts or for extended and terrifying underground through-trips. As the vale runs south the Cynfal, Goedol and Teigl come together to form the sinuous Afon Dwyryd, and the landscape softens. Wooded hills and green fields relax the eyes after the jarring industrial ruins of Blaenau, and quiet paths weave south to Llyn Trawsfynydd and the badlands of the northern Rhinogau. Buses run along the valley between Blaenau and Porthmadog.

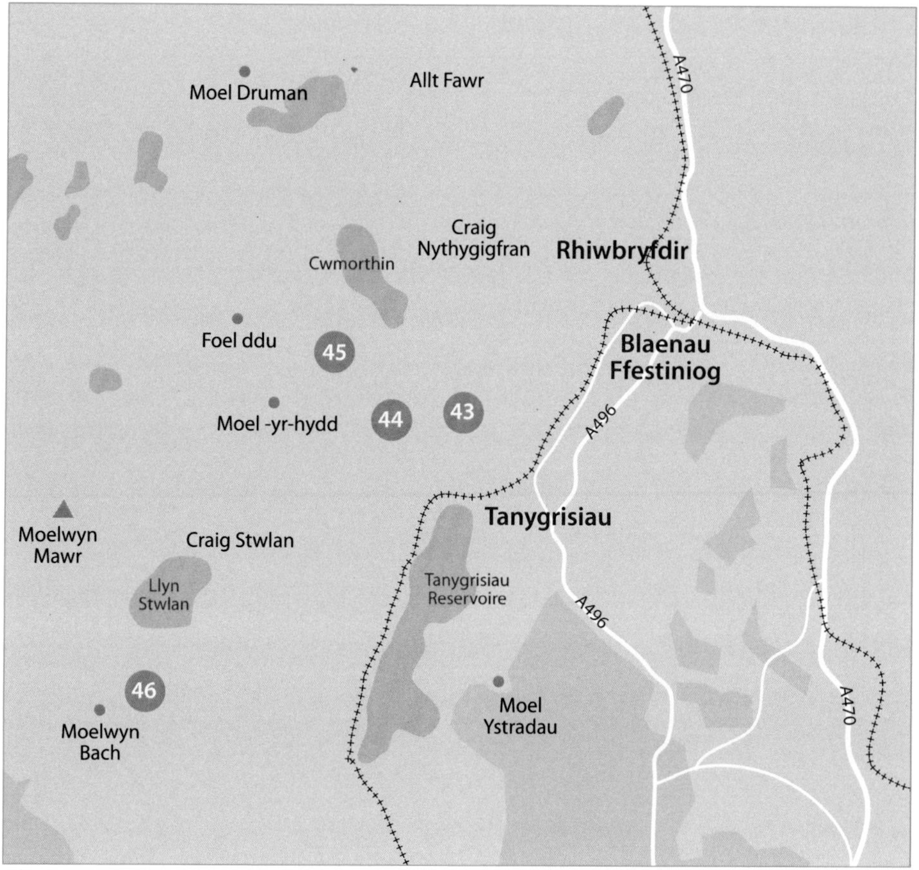
Moel Druman
Allt Fawr
A470
Craig
Nythygigfran
Rhiwbryfdir
Cwmorthin
Foel ddu
45
Blaenau
Ffestiniog
Moel -yr-hydd
44
43
A496
Tanygrisiau
Moelwyn
Mawr
Craig Stwlan
Llyn
Stwlan
Tanygrisiau
Reservoire
A496
46
Moel
Ystradau
A470
Moelwyn
Bach

43. Afon Cwmorthin (1*)

The Afon Cwmorthin runs down from Llyn Cwmorthin to the village of Tanygrisiau, just west of Blaenau Ffestiniog. The route offers a few interesting steps, coupled with interesting industrial heritage. As one of the main routes into the Moelwynion runs alongside the stream, it deserves to be more popular. The star is mainly awarded due to the unique nature of the top section of the route.

Meaning: Unknown.

Summary: Easy and escapable stream scrambling starting next to the car park. The top section runs in an open culvert and will be impassable in any kind of high water.

Conditions: The rock quality is excellent.

Height Gain: 50m

Approach: There is a car park in Tanygrisiau on the east bank of the stream at approximately SH 684454. Leave it at the north end where a path runs down to a footbridge below a waterfall. Start here.

Ascent: Climb the first step using blocks on the right side. Above this is easy clambering over boulders for some distance, until a large pool backed by a narrow waterfall is reached. On a warm day this is an enticing spot for a dip. Walk around the pool on the left, then traverse right towards the fall along a rock ledge. An easy ascent can then be made on dry, streamside rock.

Above, the stream bed is covered in slate, and a large slate wall is on the left. Walk forward as a slate wall rises on the right, beckoning you on into an open culvert (this will only be accessible in low water). A pool is soon reached, where several options present themselves. A traverse could be made above the water on the left-side slate wall. A more reasonable proposition is to spend five minutes strategically positioning some slate stepping stones to avoid the water. Some will be content to wade. If the water is too high the only option is retreat.

Beyond this is an arched bridge and another pool, best taken on the right (again, stepping stones or wet feet are the two probable outcomes). The walls have now vanished, and escape from the stream is simple.

Usual Descents: Follow the track on the east side of the stream back to the car park.

Combinations: The North-East Spur of Moel yr Hydd (route 45) makes the best continuation scramble, but Craig yr Wrysgan (route 44) is also worthwhile. Craig Nyth y Gigfran might offer a short scramble (see further scrambling opportunities). For a walking continuation, Allt Fawr can be climbed via Cwmorthin Quarry, or the Croesor-Rhosydd plateau can be accessed from the end of the cwm.

Engaging scrambling on the Afon Cwmorthin

44. Craig yr Wrysgan and Moel yr Hydd South-East Slope (1 or 2*)

Craig yr Wrysgan stands above Tanygrisiau at the entrance of Cwmorthin. It is well known to climbers escaping the bank holiday crowds of the popular Snowdonia crags, but it also offers a route for scramblers. The described scramble ascends the easy-angled side of the crag and then along the top. Traces of a path suggest that the route has a history of use. From here, a way is made through a jumbled slope of rocks and heather to reach the summit of Moel yr Hydd. The second half of the route is just one suggestion, as various ways up exist.

Meaning: Unknown, hill of the stag.

Summary: Good scrambling (avoidable and escapable) up a slabby rib, followed by pick-and-mix scrambling up a wide hillside with a choice of undefined lines.

Conditions: The rock quality is good.

Height Gain: 250m

Approach: The Afon Cwmorthin (route 43) can be used as a scrambling approach. Alternatively, from the car park in Tanygrisiau take the track on the east bank of the stream up to Cwmorthin. The route comes into view on the left, and is well seen when the track passes a stand of pine trees and a small lake (SH 681457); it climbs up the wide slabby rib beyond the lake. There is a right of way crossing the Afon Cwmorthin via a bridge here, but at the time of writing this is closed due to safety concerns. Either wade across the stream at the north end of the lake, or continue up the track to Llyn Cwmorthin, cross the stream using a bridge, and return back down the west side of the stream towards the small lake. A quarry path from the small lake crosses a leat using slate slabs and leads to the base of the rib. Various options present themselves but to stay within the grade continue to follow the path right until it passes between stone walls.

The first section of route 44

Ascent: Climb up from the extreme right end of the rib on a slabby apron of rock. Beyond this is a steeper slab, split by a runnel of heather and grass. A direct ascent on good rock and small holds is grade 2, whilst a grade 1 alternative is to move right where a very easy crack allow progress to be made. Above this the rib eases back, and the views over the precipitous left side are tremendous. Walk and scramble upwards, with the slate tips of Wrysgan quarry on the right. A small steeper step is overcome using a little gangway up the middle and more easy-angled slabs follow. At this stage on the right are the old buildings of the quarry, and several holes into the mountain side, complete with massive collapsed blocks. It is worth detouring from the scramble to have a look around the surface remains, including a peer down the steep incline which tunnels through the rock and leads back down towards Tanygrisiau (this offers an ascent/descent if care is used). From here, the scramble sticks to the crest of the rib, along a gentle mini knife edge, with the incline below. A final walk/scramble along the rib leads to a small boggy area and the vague top of the rib. This ends the first half of the scramble. From here turn right to face the upper slopes of Moel yr Hydd which is a wilderness of heather and small buttresses. Three pits have been tunnelled into the hill, and right of these is a flat area with building remains. Just to the right of the three pits is a steep grassy ramp; follow this diagonally right (faint traces of a path) past a couple of blocks, and round past a boggy area to meet a fence. Turn left and follow the fence upwards which then turns right and heads up into heather and rocks. Move up with the fence, either avoiding difficulties using a small trod, or seeking out the best scrambling on small buttresses (keep a look out for interesting rock columns). The green summit of Moel yr Hydd comes into view on the left and three options are available: 1) move left direct to the summit, past some house-sized blocks, and onto the grassy slopes; 2) keep straight up, over small final steep walls, to gain the summit ridge; 3) move right when the fence turns right, and stick with it round as it leads back towards Cwmorthin. The fence turns left and ascends a grassy gully between rocks to reach the summit ridge.

Usual descents: A pathless descent could probably be made just to the west of the rib back to Llyn Cwmorthin. Alternatively, a right of way heads back to Tanygrisiau from between Moel yr Hydd and Moelwyn Mawr.

Combinations: The best continuation is onwards over Moelwyn Mawr, Craig Ysgafn, and Moelwyn Bach (with the chance of a short scramble on Moelwyn Bach East Face – route 46), with a descent via Llyn Stwlan. Alternatively, head north over Moel Druman and Allt Fawr, followed by a descent to Cwmorthin Quarry.

The grassy ramp to start the second half of the scramble

45. North-East Spur of Moel yr Hydd (1 or 2**)

This is probably the best scramble in the Moelwynion. It rises from Llyn Cwmorthin almost to the summit of Moel yr Hydd, on delightful rock. There is a range of difficulty available and everything is avoidable by detouring to the right. Lower down the route even offers something of a Welsh rarity: friction scrambling. Although I have not seen this route described in any book, a faint path towards the top suggests that it is known by some.

Meaning: Hill of the stag.

Summary: Excellent scrambling up the slabs and steps of a defined rib.

Conditions: The rock quality is excellent.

Height Gain: 220m

Approach: A scrambling approach can be made up the Afon Cwmorthin (route 43). Otherwise, from the car park in Tanygrisiau take the track on the east bank of the stream up to Cwmorthin. Take the path on the west side of Llyn Cwmorthin to SH 677462, where slabs come down closest towards the path.

Ascent: Ascend (or avoid) the slabs by any line, which give a rare taste of friction scrambling. Keep up until a longer, stepped rib appears over towards the right. Walk across to the base of it. Climb up the rib which consists of numerous steps. Each obstacle can be taken by a variety of lines and difficulties, but the scrambling is always involving and enjoyable. Towards the top some steps are steeper and longer, and a faint path can be traced between the scrambling sections. Eventually the gradient eases, and a path can be followed beside a fence to the summit of Moel yr Hydd.

Usual Descents: A pathless descent could probably be made just to the west of the rib back to Llyn Cwmorthin. Alternatively, a right of way heads back to Tanygrisiau from between Moel yr Hydd and Moelwyn Mawr.

Combinations: The best continuation is onwards over Moelwyn Mawr, Craig Ysgafn, and Moelwyn Bach (with the chance of a short scramble on Moelwyn Bach East Face – route 46), with a descent via Llyn Stwlan. Alternatively, head north over Moel Druman and Allt Fawr, followed by a descent to Cwmorthin Quarry.

1. Scrambling against a backdrop of slate; 2. Will Farrelly, Dave Jackson and Susan Peacock on the North East Spur of the Moel yr Hydd; 3. The starting slabs.

46. Moelwyn Bach East Face (1 or 2)

The east side of Moelwyn Bach consists of an easy angled area of slabby rocks. Although short, this route offers a fun scramble to the summit if approaching from Llyn Stwlan.

Meaning: Little white hill.

Summary: A short route with a choice of line, topping out on a summit.

Conditions: The rock quality is excellent.

Height Gain: 40m

Approach: Numerous approaches can be made to Llyn Stwlan from Tanygrisiau, the quickest being along the access road that runs below Clogwyn yr Oen and Clogwyn y Bustach to the Llyn Stwlan dam. If approaching in this way, some brief scrambling can be enjoyed on small slabs on the little hillock of Carreg Blaen Llym (SH 666442), just beyond the dam. From Llyn Stwlan/Carreg Blaen Llym proceed south along a very faint path to a quarry carved into the hill, and slate tip at SH 663438. If approaching from one of the scrambles on Moel yr Hydd there are two options: 1) to continue from Moel yr Hydd over Moelwyn Mawr and down to Bwlch Stwlan; 2) to take the traversing quarry track from the bwlch between Moel yr Hydd and Moelwyn Mawr. This traverses around the west side of Llyn Stwlan and leads to Bwlch Stwlan. For either route, continue from Bwlch Stwlan on the traversing quarry path (now just a trod) which runs under steep ground and past quartz rocks to arrive at the start of the scramble.

Ascent: The route ascends to the right of the quarry, but to the left of steeper ground identified by quartz rocks at the base. Scramble upwards towards the top, with a choice of line. The scrambling is over all too quickly, and after a short walk the summit cairn appears.

Approaching the rocks of Moelwyn Bach East Face

Usual Descents: From a cairn, a well-used slate path runs down in a northerly direction towards Llyn Stwlan.

Combinations: The obvious continuation is over Moelwyn Mawr and Moel yr Hydd.

The Vale of Ffestiniog – Further Scrambling Opportunities

There may be more scrambling to be had on Moel yr Hydd, overlooking Llyn Cwmorthin. Certainly there is a least one interesting looking gully line. It also seems likely that there may be more stream scrambles in the area, possibly at the head of Cwm Croesor. Craig Nyth y Gigfran guards the opposite entrance of Cwmorthin to Craig yr Wrysgan and rests upon an ocean of slate waste. It appears that a short scramble might be contrived up its left side (SH 682459) which would lead to the crag summit, perhaps followed by a walk to Allt Fawr.

The Afon Prysor is a fine river that originates in a boggy expanse of moorland before flowing down a cwm of the same name and entering Llyn Trawsfynydd. Beyond the reservoir damn it enters the lengthy Ceunant Llennyrch Gorge. Here is a land of ferns and mushrooms, of mosses and of crumbling gorge walls. The gorge is popular with outdoor groups who descend it, but few experience it in ascent. It is possible to proceed some way up the gorge, mainly by wading or swimming through pools, with little actual scrambling. However, this is one of the richest sites for oceanic liverworts and mosses in Wales. Careful liaison with groups has avoided potential damage to the species that grow here, but this is probably not a site to visit solo, and so I would advise that this site is left alone.

About two miles east from the Afon Prysor is the Afon Tafarn Helyg. This runs in a deep ravine named the Ceunant Llechrwd next to the A487. It may be a simple walk, or a deadly scramble, but it is probably an atmospheric sort of place (apart from any noise from the main road), although the gorge is not in access land. Nearby is the Afon Cynfal that runs for some distance in a wooded gorge, heading east from Pont Tal-y-Bont (SH 687415). This is probably canyoning territory, but footpaths and access land would facilitate a closer look. The gorge culminates in the impressive

Rhaeadr y Cwm (SH 739417) that falls from the edge of the Migneint. An ascent of this waterfall would almost certainly be outside the realm of the scrambler, but a sojourn up to its base might be feasible.

On the north side of the Afon Dwyryd is Plas Tan-y-Bwlch (the Snowdonia National Park Environmental Studies Centre). The land here is, without question, perfectly idyllic. The Afon Dwyryd winds through the valley; still and unhurried, whilst flycatchers flit through the oak woods. Even the steam from the trains on the Ffestiniog Railway brings to mind bygone days of simpler pleasures. Hidden in the woods are three gorges. Two cannot be climbed, and the other features multiple unsolvable waterfalls, but when combined they make a worthwhile day out in a neglected area. There is a small car park on the shore of Llyn Mair (SH 652414). Walk east along the north shore of the lake, past the houses and a track on the right. The road turns left, and beyond this take a right into the woods. The path crosses between the mill pond and the head of the Llyn Mair gorge. On the other side turn left to descend on a path next to the gorge. This can be followed down. Alternatively, look out for some old red wooden stakes. They mark an old path that keeps closer to the gorge edge, and lead to a platform with good views of waterfalls in the gorge. The gorge itself is impressive, being a deep, incised ravine full of lush vegetation. The path reaches the road to Plas Tan-y-Bwlch; turn left here to reach a bridge at the bottom of the Llyn Mair Gorge. A small path runs into the gorge through a clump of bamboo on the upstream side. However, there is no point in attempting an ascent as there are numerous waterfalls that cannot be climbed. Additionally, footfall would disturb the copious layers of moss and other plants that cling to the boulders and gorge walls.

A walk north-east through woodland leads to a house at the base of the Coed Bronturnor Gorge (grade 1) (SH 666414). This gorge features lots of waterfalls that cannot be climbed, along with some short traverses and scrambling. If followed, it leads out to the Ffestiniog Railway and the cottage at Coed-y-Bleiddiau station. A look at the map reveals that the nearby outflow of Llyn y Garnedd flows through a gorge (SH 664418). This can be reached by crossing the Ffestiniog Railway (go under using the tunnel the stream flows through). The stream enters on the left. Beyond a couple of waterfalls and pools (and a mine adit on the left) a step is reached where the water falls on the left side, below a rhododendron. This can be climbed using dry, unfriendly rock on the right side to enter a narrow, claustrophobic trough. At the end of this is a waterfall barring progress, and escape is impossible on either side of the trough. The only option is to retreat back down the unfriendly step, which is not an appealing option. For this reason, the upper trough is probably best left alone. From below the unfriendly step, escape can be made on the north side by a wall. There is a very faint path above this that follows the gorge, but this soon makes a suicidal-looking traverse across vegetation above the ravine and is also best ignored. A more restful option is to follow the valley that runs north-east from the Coed-y-Bleiddiau station towards the Nant Ystradau. There is a small path (not marked on the map) that leads the way into this lovely pass. At around SH 667423 the view ahead opens up by some ruins. Moving left here gains a forest track that leads to Llyn y Garnedd, and then to the Croesor - Llyn Mair road. The starting point is just beyond.

Not far again from this location is the small village of Rhyd. The Afon Rhyd runs in a deep, wooded ravine that always piques my curiosity when I drive past. There is no access land here, but a right of way leads to the start of the gorge at SH 621417. I would be very interested to find out what lies within the ravine.

1. One of the many unclimable falls in the Coed Bronturnor Gorge;
2. Warning sign in the Afon Prysor.

Glyn Lledr (Lledr Valley) and the Migneint

Scenic Glyn Lledr runs from the Crimea Pass down to Betws-y-Coed as a mixture of pasture and woodland, with its namesake river flowing peacefully past pretty sounding places: Roman Bridge, Dolwyddelan, Pont-y-Pant. To its north and west it is bounded by the Moelwynion and Moel Siabod which dominates the area from here (a startling contrast to its grassy lifeless profile from the north). To the south lie the forgotten Ffestiniog Hills of Moel Penamnen and Y Ro Wen. A handful of scrambles can be accessed from the valley, with public transport being provided by rail or bus.

For the sake of this book, the Migneint is also included in this section. The Migneint lies about five miles south-east of Glyn Lledr. It is one of the great blanket bogs of Wales; a vast, relatively trackless wilderness of heather, grass and rushes. It sprawls for quiet miles until the squat shape of Arenig Fach rises up to punctuate the bleakness. Several scrambles are found on the Migneint, which should satisfy those who grow weary of the tourist crowds of Snowdonia.

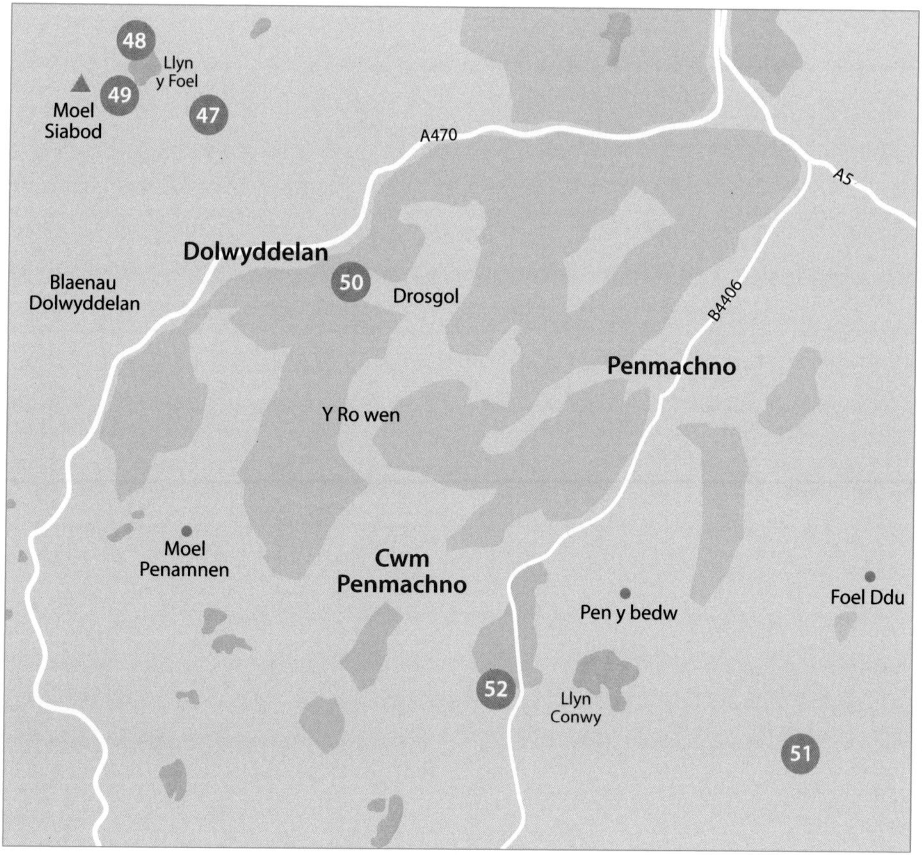
48
Llyn
y Foel
49
Moel
Siabod
47
A470
A5
Dolwyddelan
50
Drosgol
Blaenau
Dolwyddelan
B4406
Penmachno
Y Ro wen
Moel
Penamnen
Cwm
Penmachno
Foel Ddu
Pen y bedw
52
Llyn
Conwy
51

47. Afon Ystumiau (1)

The best approach to Moel Siabod is undoubtedly from Dolwyddelan. From here there is none of the dull grassiness of its north-western slopes, and a much more rugged land is found. For those travelling this way, the described scramble offers some frivolity.

Meaning: Meandering river.

Summary: Scrambling up a forest stream tangled with deadwood, followed by more open scrambling.

Conditions: The rock is slimy to begin with, but improves slightly above the forest. Since this route was first visited, it appears that much (all?) of the forest has been felled. It is unknown how this might have affected the gorge; increased light may have reduced the sliminess of the rocks.

Height Gain: 230m (includes sections of walking)

Approach: The obvious approach is from Dolwyddelan, where there is a small car park at the station. Walk north up the small lane to the left of Y Gwydyr pub, then turn right at the end along another lane. After 70m, take a footpath on the left which leads through fields and into the forest. From here turn left onto a forest track and follow this, ignoring any side tracks, until it crosses the Afon Ystumiau at SH 732543. Beyond here, take a track on the left, and then a fork right. Ignore another track on the right, and continue to reach a footbridge at SH 724544 where a path runs into the clear-felled forest. This can alternatively be reached by taking a track from Capel Tan-y-Garth (SH 736567) just outside of Capel Curig. This leads over moorland and down into the forest.

Ascent: The Afon Ystumiau lies adjacent to the forest path. The first notable waterfall is guarded by a deep pool. There is no way to traverse the walls so avoid this by walking round on the left. Above, rejoin the stream and climb a slimy short wall on the right. From here progress is made more interesting by the constant presence of branches and deadwood hanging into the channel. The next worthwhile section is a short, tricky traverse down the left wall, with a large boulder to the right.

More ducking, weaving and scrambling gains the largest fall yet. Above this, escape is made via a stile to more open ground reminiscent of the Rhinogau.

1. On the Afon Ystumiau before the forest was felled; 2. The upper section of the route.

Walking beside the stream leads to a two-tier waterfall. This is first climbed on the right to arrive below the upper fall. An energetic escape through boulders is then made on the left side. Easy ground leads on. Across another flat piece of land a bouldery gully can be spied. Ignore this and take the right branch of the stream at the fork. Follow the stream, enjoying some brief clambering on rock on its right side to arrive below the final rise. First, dispatch an easy-angled slimy slab then take a direct line on the left sticking to the water. A stone dam/wall and the awe-inspiring Cwm y Foel then come into view.

Usual Descents: A path beside the stream leads back to the forest.

Combinations: From this side of Llyn y Foel Embryo Ridge (route 48) shows off its rocky but vague line and offers one continuation. The Daear Ddu ridge (grade 1 – route 49) on the left side of the cwm is another option to the summit of Moel Siabod. The best return to Dolwyddelan from the summit is down the west ridge and then on to Carnedd y Cribau. Paths and tracks then head east down to Roman Bridge.

48. Embryo Ridge, Moel Siabod (1)

Embryo Ridge is Moel Siabod's lost scramble. It received a short mention in early editions of Scrambles in Snowdonia as a grade 2 and a target for "confirmed scramblers" but was subsequently removed (presumably because the book only covers Yr Wyddfa, Eifionydd, Carneddau and Glyderau). Daear Ddu (Siabod's east ridge) is a popular grade 1 scramble that bookends one end of the rocky nameless cwm, and Embryo Ridge marks the other end. The scrambling is short and the line vague from below, but it offers a fresh and quiet way to the summit for jaded scramblers.

Summary: A short scramble up an untrodden ridge. This author has lowered the grade from 2 to 1.

Conditions: The rock is rough.

Height Gain: 140m

Approach: The best approach is from Dolwyddelan, using forest tracks to reach the footpath at SH 724544 which then leads to Llyn y Foel, or scramble the Afon Ystumiau (route 47) as a start to the day. At Llyn y Foel go around the lake on the east side, aiming for Embryo Ridge that vaguely bounds the right side of the cwm. The more popular approach is from Pont-Cyfyng (SH 734570), taking the footpath past Rhos. This leads past Llyn y Rhos (unnamed on maps, this name comes from "The Lakes of Eryri") to the Foel Quarry and cliff-backed pool (SH 717555). A path then climbs to the col overlooking Llyn y Foel. Embryo Ridge lies at the right of the cwm, beside Embryo Gully; an obvious couloir (though this is not visible if taking the second approach). Start at SH 714549, well right of the couloir, and right of the scree patches on the hillside.

Ascent: From below, the line of the ridge is vague and wide. To keep within grade 1 terrain stay well right away from the couloir, aiming for a wide rock tier that is visible up the slope (a direct ascent alongside the couloir is much harder). Walk up heather and bilberry to this first main step (scrambling a couple of other small steps on the way) and climb it wherever. Above this the view ahead reveals more. Simply scramble up picking the best rock. By moving far left some exposure can be found dropping away into Embryo Gully until the ridge runs out on Siabod's slabby summit ridge.

Having come this far it would be a shame to miss out on the summit so head left (south-west). This involves first avoiding the notch at the top of Embryo Gully. It is then a matter of scrambling along the rocky flat ridge to the summit trig point.

Usual Descents: To return to Capel Curig a path leads north-east to the forest and Plas y Brenin, though in poor visibility the start of it can be difficult to find. Those returning to Dolwyddelan can down-scramble Daear Ddu (route 49) and retrace their outward route. Another option is to move west from the summit and descend a vague spur south to Dolwyddelan Reservoir (SH 697530), taking care to avoid the crag of Craig Ddu on the way. Forest tracks can then be followed back to the road.

Combinations: This is where those who started in Dolwyddelan can enjoy a full mountain day. Descend the west ridge of Moel Siabod and climb Carnedd y Cribau. Beyond this (SH 666523) a right of way leads back east to the Lledr Valley. To extend the walk further, continue over Moel Meirch and past peaceful Llyn Edno, and descend over Yr Arddu back to the road. Tigers could ignore the Yr Arddu escape and proceed on over the triple summits of Ysgafell Wen, then on again to Moel Druman and Allt Fawr, finishing out to Llyn Dyrnogydd and to Bwlch y Gorddinan (Crimea Pass). It may be possible to get a bus (or hitch a lift) to Dolwyddelan, but the walk back to the road head at Blaenau Dolwyddelan is a pleasant end to the day. From here, there is a pleasant path to Dolwyddelan that runs from the house at Bertheos (SH 719513). This long circuit is a good 16 miles or so.

Embryo Ridge is the vague line to the right of the gully that runs up to the skyline notch

49. Daear Ddu Ridge (1**)

The Daear Ddu Ridge is one of the most popular ascent routes on Moel Siabod, and rightly so. It is an elegant line, bounding one side of a mountain cwm, and the scrambling is interesting and on good rock. The route is well known so only the briefest of description is given here. The best approach is from Dolwyddelan, using forest tracks to reach the footpath at SH 724544 which then leads to Llyn y Foel, or scramble the Afon Ystumiau (route 47) as a start to the day. From Llyn y Foel, Daear Ddu ascends the left side of the cwm, starting at approximately SH 712544. The ascent is mostly obvious, and a path threads a way upwards. Generally, moving to the right leads to rocks overlooking the cwm (exposure here if desired), and moving to the left allows a friendlier way to be found. A variety of exact routes can be taken, so a detailed description isn't warranted. For those who want to up the grade, there are more difficult steps that can be sought out. Higher up the sustained rocky section ends (at a notch if you have been following the right edge) and a broad shoulder of hill takes over. It is possible to seek out further scrambling here, and those who enjoy exposure will again stick to the right edge. When the scrambling runs out, the summit trig point is nearby. Descent and combinations are as for Embryo Ridge (route 48).

1. The elegant line of Daear Ddu Ridge;
2. Susan Peacock scrambling on Daear Ddu.

50. Afon Bwlch y Groes (1)

Dolwyddelan is a village that ticks all the right boxes – a river runs through it, there are gentle pastures beside the road, and it is overlooked by the gentle faces of Moel Siabod and Y Ro Wen. Equally, it is overlooked by the tourists. On the south side of the village, a track heads off up Y Ro Wen, and beside this is a pleasant stream which offers a short diversion for those in the area.

Meaning: River of the pass of the cross.

Summary: Easy and escapable scrambling followed by walking in a small gorge.

Conditions: The rock is quite slippery, and socks over boots are recommended.

Height Gain: 90m

Approach: There is parking (signed) in Dolwyddelan over the bridge at SH 737521. Walk over the railway bridge and turn left up the street. At the top the lane turns left, but continue ahead, keeping the Afon Bwlch y Groes on the right and a house on the left until the path enters a field beyond a small gate.

Ascent: Gain the stream bed and follow it with ease. It turns right and two mossy waterslides are best avoided. Slink through the branches of a tree that crosses the stream to where the channel 'splits'. The right side is a short steep fall, so scramble up the left side. Climb a second step to find a narrow trough backed by a waterfall – there is no continuation here so escape on the left. The next obstacle is another intimidating fall that could perhaps be climbed (first up the left, then switch to the right) but is better bypassed. Above, it appears that the scramble is over, but a short distance further on the stream flows in an atmospheric little gorge. Walk up this to find another waterfall that cannot be climbed. There is a slanting ledge to the right of the gorge but do not be tempted by this – the ground is very loose and insecure. Instead turn right and clamber up to the fence, where a small path leads on. There is another optional step above the waterfall, and the track can be gained just to the left of the stream.

Usual Descents: The track leads quickly back to Dolwyddelan.

Combinations: The summit of Y Ro Wen can be gained by following the track. From there, a continuation over Foel Fras and Moel Penamnen is a natural route, and one that few people follow. Either descend into Cwm Penamnen and walk out, or go down to Roman Bridge where a path can be followed back to the start. Another, even less walked route, is to ignore Y Ro Wen and head north-east over Drosgol to Foel Felen, where a path leads down to Pont-y-Pant. The heather does make for tough going, however.

The mossy world of the Afon Bwlch y Groes

51. Afon Conwy – Migneint Section (3**)

Three miles or so after leaving its namesake lake, the infant Afon Conwy enters a wild gorge and tumbles down through deep pools and under chossy cliffs, before calming and flowing through Ysbyty Ifan. The gorge is adjacent to the B4407 across the Migneint, but this is not Tourist Country, and those journeying by speed on their way. A visit to the gorge is demanding and involves interesting scrambling, plus lots of deep wading and occasional swimming. Dangerous potholes and undercut walls abound below the water level meaning this trip should not be trifled with. Drought conditions and buoyancy aids are recommended. This route took three hours to cover a distance just over 1km.

Meaning: Reedy river or river of the bogs.

Summary: A time-consuming trip first down and then up a large gorge, involving interesting scrambling and deep pools. The given grade is awarded for the seriousness of the trip, not the technicality of the scrambling.

Conditions: Care is needed with slippery rock (both above and below the water). The peaty water is very dark which makes gauging the depth of pools very difficult indeed.

Height Gain: 70m (1km horizontal traversing distance)

Approach: A couple of cars can be parked opposite the drive to the Llyn Conwy water treatment works (SH 809453), but be mindful not to block passing places. An approach from below the point where the Afon Conwy and Afon Serw join would be useful, but there are no rights of way or access land. A right of way leaves the B4407 at SH 814456 and leads to a bridge over the river. It was hoped to be possible to cross this and descend to the point where the rivers join, but steep banks of vegetation prevent this. Instead, access must be made at the bridge. An optional short jaunt downstream gives a taste of the lower gorge, before a return to the bridge is made, and the upper gorge explored.

Ascent: Enter the gorge and move downstream, wading and clambering. Soon, a ledge system is reached on the left hand side of a pool. At first glance this seems like a dead end but progress is possible by two routes; one dry and one wet. For the dry: walk to the end of the ledges and climb straight up and through a heather shrub to arrive below a tree. A downsloping ledge then regains the river below the deep part of the pool. For the wet: carefully lower off the ledge into the pool. It is very deep, but there are a few submerged rocks. Cautious progress can then be made along the edge of the pool. Be warned that the cliff here is severely undercut under the water line which could potentially create dangerous currents.

Move down below an impressively overhung cliff high on the left wall to reach a boulder choke. Climb down this on the left to reach a steep waterslide. It might be possible to bypass this on the boulder to the right, but re-ascent might then be impossible. In light of this, turn around and retrace the route back to the bridge. Approach the bridge on the right side (facing upstream). Lower in off a ledge, and a crossing can then be made to the left hand side by wading (there is a shallower part that can hopefully be glimpsed through the peaty water). Go under the bridge to another pool and cross back to the right. Wade along below the bridge or traverse a foot ledge, then avoid the pool by climbing upwards into the woodland. The river bed can not be regained ahead, so turn around and escape back over a fence to the bridge. Obviously, this last section under the bridge could have been completely avoided, but where's the fun in that?

Cross the bridge to the side away from the road and climb up to the top of the bank. Where feasible, descend easy slopes to the river bed. The next obstacle is a pretty waterfall flowing over a lip. This can be tackled on its right hand side. Beyond this the gorge continues, and challenges include various awkward traverses and interesting scrambling. One pool offers no traverse, and the best method of progression is to enter the water at its far end and battle up over a cascade approximately one foot high; even this measly fall is quite strong! Another memorable fall is best tackled on the right by crawling a few feet along a tight ledge.

Keep upwards, avoiding or tackling obstacles and falls as they come, and eventually the gorge relaxes. It appears to be the end, but continue on and the gorge builds itself back up again. A waterfall enters on the right. Another surprisingly tricky bit is a 7ft wall sticking into a pool that must be overcome. Soon beyond this another pool is encountered. Wading is possible along the right side until shallow ground terminates before a black and scary large water-worn pothole. This does not look appealing. On the first trip a retreat was made here, and escape made on the left side (looking up) via a mossy slab and steep vegetation. This bank emerged opposite the drive for the water works.

When practical rejoin the gorge bed. Here are more sculptured holes and deep pools that seem filled with malice and danger. Most are best avoided until the gorge finally relents. Escape and return to the car.

Usual Descents: N/A

Combinations: A day spent wandering the peaty nothingness of the Migneint might appeal to lovers of solitude. For those in need of another fix, the Afon y Foel (route 52) is a short drive away.

1. *The boulder choke;*
2. *Unorthodox moves on the Afon Conwy.*

2

52. Afon y Foel (2*)

The drive onto the Migneint from Penmachno is through Cwm Hafodyredwydd; a place of plantations and solitude. As the road cuts above the head of the cwm a river can be spied down below as it spills over large slabs. This is the Afon y Foel. Above the slabs but unglimpsed from above is a narrow and interesting gorge section (the Ceunant Mawr).

Meaning: River of the bare hill.

Summary: Slippery scrambling up easy angled slabs followed by the ascent of a narrow and mossy ravine.

Conditions: The lower slabs are treacherous; perhaps the worst I have encountered. Socks over boots are a must.

Height Gain: 90m

Approach: There is room to park one car on grass at Pont Elen (SH 765457) at the head of the cwm. From here walk down the road until the cattle grid and plantation is reached (SH 767464), and where a track slants back left and down into the cwm to the Afon y Foel.

Ascent: Climb the stream, which is wide at first. The angle is easy but the slabs are extremely slippery. Sticking to the course of the water offers the best rock, as the power of the water lessens the slime. Successive water slides are separated by pools.

Above the slabs the river runs through a tight and narrow gorge. Wade and traverse pools until a larger step is reached. The rocks to the left look unsafe, so climb up through the water directly, and exit left above. Next comes more wading and traversing. One pool is backed by a large boulder, with a mini chute and lodged little chockstone to its left. A large mossy waterfall appears which is clearly too difficult. Leave the gorge on the left. The ground is steep and unpleasant, so slant back, climbing above the ravine to easy ground. Once above the gorge cross a minor tributary then head down easy slopes back into the gorge. There is a

Chris Peacock in the upper ravine of the Afon y Foel

surprisingly baffling little step that can be overcome by sitting on the right side with feet on the left, and 'walking' up. Further up another waterfall is reached; this one overhanging. Vacate the gorge on the left to emerge behind the cottage of Hafodyredwydd and return to the car.

Combinations: The Conwy gorge (route 51) is a short drive/walk away (3.6 miles if taking the right of way across the Migneint).

Glyn Lledr and the Migneint – Further Scrambling Opportunities

Scrambling opportunities elsewhere in the valley appear somewhat limited. The very bottom section of the Afon Cwm Penamnen (SH 736518) above Dolwyddelan might provide some brief entertainment. Even if not, Cwm Penamnen is a surprisingly lovely place to wander. Despite the forestry plantation a walk along the single track road to nowhere is delightful. It passes woodland and pasture, and the burbling river adds to the peaceful, sleepy atmosphere.

Further along the Lledr Valley is the Ceunant y Garnedd, above Roman Bridge at SH 701522. That may be worth a closer look. Beyond here are the twin lakes of Llynau Diwaunedd (SH 684537), quiet and unfrequented, and above the water is Carnedd y Cribau, suddenly looking very mountainous indeed. A determined scrambler might find some rock here on the hill's east face; they would certainly find solitude. Not far away there is a short ravine marked below Moel Lledr at SH 683490, to the north of Allt Fawr. Anyone wanting to investigate it might have to suffer a boggy walk in, but I imagine the solitude would provide ample compensation. To the east of Bwlch y Gorddinan (Crimea Pass) is the pleasant top of Moel Farlwyd (SH 707487). There is a little scrappy scrambling to be had when leaving this hill to ascend adjacent Moel Penamnen.

The sweeping desolation of the Migneint is punctuated by numerous small hills, of which the finest is perhaps Y Gamallt. Its long summit ridge bristles with crags, whilst below two lakes are cradled in shelter. It falls under Hewitt height, however, and so it remains a quiet place. Despite its cragginess, there is little for the scrambler bar a 20m clamber up to the summit ridge at approximately SH 751442. A determined investigator may find more to go at, but others will be happy to wander along, perhaps also summiting nearby Y Garnedd.

The Afon Serw may provide some scrambling and wading where it joins the Afon Conwy (SH 816454) but as mentioned under the Afon Conwy description, getting down to the river here is difficult due to steep slopes and vegetation. Just below the Migneint at Cwm Penmachno there are some enticing ravines. The Dyfnant flows down a ravine named Ceunant Blaen y Cwm at SH 755480. An approach could be made using the right of way to Hafod Fraith Uchaf and then a forest track and access land used to head back to the ravine. From across the valley it seems that there might be at least one fall that cannot be climbed, but the ravine looks very promising and may hold a real gem of a gorge. A short distance up the valley is the oddly named Nant Beti Richards, but this seems steeper and an ascent may not be feasible. There is also an open stream, nameless on the OS map, that flows into Cwm Penmachno from the south-west. It runs to the east side of the quarry from an old dam at SH 748464 and looks like it might give an easy and escapable scramble.

Ceunant Blaen y Cwm

Clocaenog and Mynydd Hiraethog

Clocaenog Forest is a vast expanse, primarily consisting of monotonous conifer plantation. Mountain bikers explore the areas around Llyn Brenig and Llyn Alwen, as do a few walkers, but most of the forest is quiet and empty. On a hazy autumn afternoon, the atmosphere can be strangely melancholic, with the swish of the wind turbines adding an eerie drone to the air. In the west the forest ends and Mynydd Hiraethog continues. Mynydd Hiraethog roughly translates as the moors of longing, but is also known as the Denbigh Moors. Only one full scramble is described here.

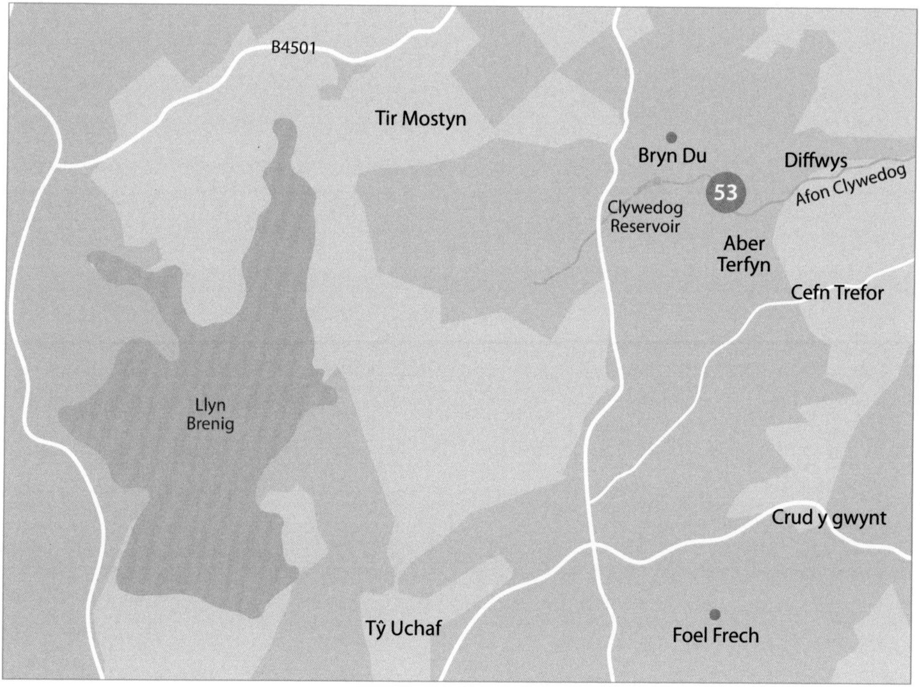
B4501
Tir Mostyn
Bryn Du
Diffwys
53
Afon Clywedog
Clywedog Reservoir
Aber Terfyn
Cefn Trefor
Llyn Brenig
Crud y gwynt
Tŷ Uchaf
Foel Frech

53. Afon Clywedog (Ceunant Diffwys)

The aforementioned dullness of the forest is punctuated by highlights, one of which is the incised ravine of Ceunant Diffwys, formed where the infant Afon Clywedog leaves the pretty Clywedog Reservoir (not to be confused with the much larger Llyn Clywedog reservoir in mid Wales). The steep side-slopes of the gorge are an impressive 100m high where the river enters the pasture land. An ascent offers a real adventure, though there is almost no actual scrambling; most of the route consists of avoiding cascades using steep and unstable vegetation, and as such, the route can not be graded using conventional means. This is no place for novices.

Meaning: Wild, rocky river (ravine of the precipice).

Summary: A trip up a large gorge, with waterfalls generally bypassed on loose vegetation. For the lower section there is no escape, but further on the difficulties ease and escape can be made via the right hand slopes.

Conditions: An ascent of the first major obstacle is only possible with socks over boots (though it can be avoided). The rock is slippery, and much of it is loose. The vegetation on the banks is primarily moss, bracken, trees and brambles, and numerous trees must be battled through.

Height Gain: 120m (1km traverse)

Approach: On the first ascent the approach attempts were as epic as the gorge itself. After parking up on the minor road through the forest (lots of space at SJ 009555) an attempt was made to force through the undergrowth beyond the end of the track at SJ 018571. After overcoming a gorse thicket we came to steep slopes on the south side of the gorge – no way down. Undeterred we tried to descend the nearby stream of the Aber Terfyn. This was precarious enough, but became dangerous when the angle steepened and numerous small falls presented themselves. Our final

Struggling with slippery rock on the lower waterfall on the Afon Clywedog

ingenious solution was to leave the stream and head east towards the fields of Pen y Graig. After bashing through the undergrowth we duly arrived at the fence and (shamefully) hopped it to continue our journey as trespassers, off the access land. We re-crossed the Aber Terfyn, cut through another field, hopped another fence, and slid down to reach the Afon Clywedog, once more safe on the access land. Such an approach cannot be recommended. A better bet is to start from the car park on the north side of Llyn Clywedog at SJ 010575, and walk east, using the track on the north bank of the ravine. Once near the farm of Diffwys, head back to the start of the ravine at SJ 021573, being sure to keep to the access land, and not the private farm track. This will probably involve some vegetation-bashing, but best consider it a warm-up for the jungle ahead.

Ascent: Follow the Afon Clywedog, across flat ground. Progress is made on either bank, or in the shallow stream itself. At one point the right bank is host to a scree slope of slatey-rock – further up the gorge there is vegetation growing on such stuff; not a reassuring thought. Soon the first waterfall is reached. It is quite a scene, nestling below vegeted banks, and seen by few people. It can be climbed on ledges to the left of the water, but this is impossible without the security of socks over boots. It can also be avoided by moving diagonally left from the river, then back across right to arrive above the fall.

More jungle-bashing leads to another series of cascades. The first one is climbed using rock and vegetation on the left side, as is the next smaller step. Beyond, the second waterfall is reached, taller than the first, and with a deep-looking plunge pool at its base. Admire the scene, then grit your teeth. Progress is made on the left hand slopes, by scrabbling up through moss and undergrowth. There is another smaller fall above the large one, so do not descend to the river too early. Instead, keep up and along through trees and bracken; a rope or some long slings may be useful for this section to provide security for followers, but be sure to use solid, growing trees, not rotting dead ones. Once beyond the falls the river can be re-joined at some grassy sections. The difficulties are now over.

From here the atmosphere changes as the trees thin out. Bracken and heather dominate the side slopes. Just before the river turns left there is a short traverse where the water flows in a rocky runnel, then some very easy scrambling if the rocky bed is stuck to. The trees close back in, and more very easy steps lead to the dam at the reservoir. Leave the stream on the right side.

Scrambling up the second waterfall

Usual Descents: N/A

Combinations: There are numerous tracks and paths through the forest allowing a full day of walking to be had after the gorge.

Clocaenog and Mynydd Hiraethog – Further Scrambling Opportunities

The map hints at a couple of other gorges in the forest. One is the Oernant at SJ 020557, and the other is the Ceunant Nilig at SJ 026552. Access land provides a way in to both. There is also a waterfall (SH 989523) near Tal y Cefn Isaf that would provide a few minutes of scrambling if passing. Beyond the forest onto Mynydd Hiraethog there is a gorge at the outflow of the Aled Isaf Reservoir. The waterfall here is named Rhaeadr y Bedd (SH 916599). Further downstream the Afon Aled flows in a ravine. Further west again is the Afon Cledwen (SH 875578) which appears to have some waterfalls at its upper end.

The waterfall near Tal y Cefn Isaf

The Rhinogau and Arenig

The Rhinogau (often called the Rhinogs, but properly the Rhinogau or Rhinogydd) are the rough mountains of Wales. The main ridge forms an undulating backbone from the Vale of Ffestiniog all the way to Dolgellau, and is punctuated by thrilling highlights. The badlands and canyons of Diffwys and Foel Penolau in the north; the vast bulk of Rhinog Fawr from Bwlch Drws Ardudwy (is it really only 720m?); the exciting dome of Rhinog Fach; then the long and undulating ridge down from the highpoint of Y Llethr. The two sides of the range also show different characters. To the west is the sparkling expanse of Cardigan Bay, whilst the east is consumed by forested fingers of the mighty Coed y Brenin. And yet, despite these glories, a day can be had wandering the range when not a single person is encountered. Ah well, all the more undiscovered scrambles to discover.

The range can be accessed using public transport from the east (there is a bus route along the A470) and west (rail link from Porthmadog to Abermaw/Barmouth, and bus from Ffestiniog to Abermaw/Barmouth), with numerous villages to select as a convenient base. There is also a useful bothy hiding in the area.

As for the Arenig, when people talk of them they usually mean the two so-named peaks; Arenig Fawr and Arenig Fach. Indeed, this is justified as both are fine mountains, coupled with the added bonus of solitude, as neither is a popular peak. The full Arenig range extends over a much larger area, however. It is bordered in the north-west by the great peaty desolation of the Migneint, truly the wilderness of North Wales. The west is marked by the A470 from Trawsfynydd to Dolgellau, and the east by Llyn Tegid (Bala Lake) and the A494. This vast area withholds eight Hewitts. Naturally, scrambles are thin on the ground when compared with the land of plenty further north, but there is fun to be found, provided you look in the right place. These are not routes to be done in

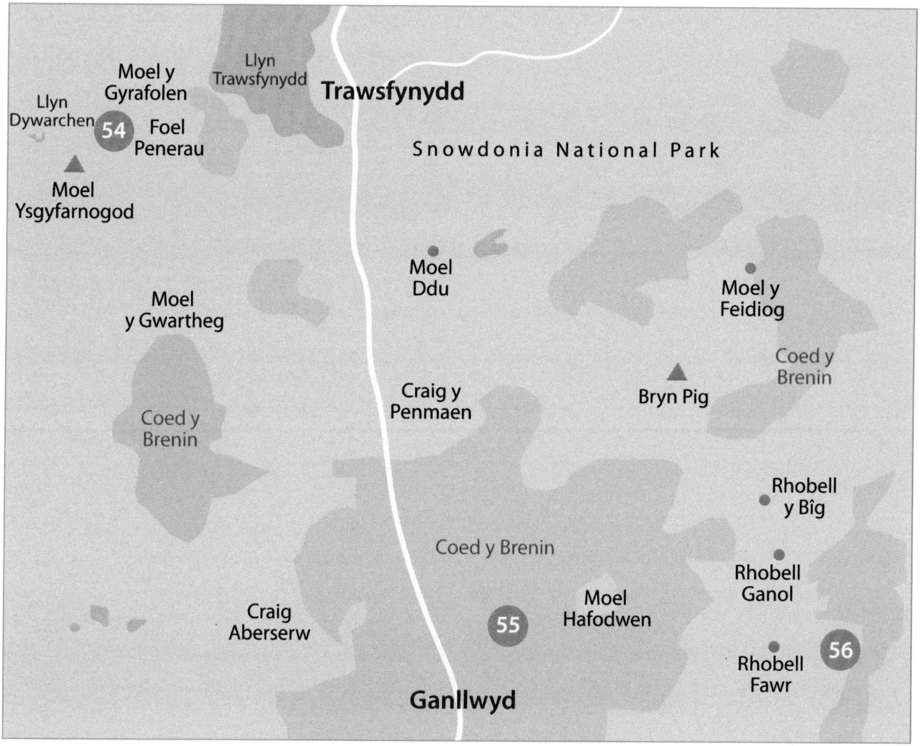
Moel y
Gyrafolen
Llyn
Trawsfynydd
Trawsfynydd
Llyn
Dywarchen
54
Foel
Penerau
Snowdonia National Park
Moel
Ysgyfarnogod
Moel
Ddu
Moel y
Feidiog
Moel
y Gwartheg
Coed y
Brenin
Craig y
Penmaen
Bryn Pig
Coed y
Brenin
Rhobell
y Bîg
Coed y Brenin
Rhobell
Ganol
Moel
Hafodwen
Craig
Aberserw
55
56
Rhobell
Fawr
Ganllwyd

their own right, but are best enjoyed (like most scrambles) as part of a longer mountain day.

A bus serves the western side of the range on the A470, and the T3 (Abermaw/ Barmouth to Wrexham) journeys along the A494 in the east. Unfortunately, it is impossible to access the northern Arenig by public transport from the A4212, unless some day the Bala-Ffestiniog railway is resurrected. We can but dream.

1. The Rhinogau from Craig y Penmaen; 2. Rhinog Fach across Llyn Hywel.

2

54. The Northern Rhinogau – Moel y Gyrafolen to Moel Ysgyfarnogod (1)

If the central Rhinogau are neglected, then what does that make Moel Ysgyfarnogod and its companions at the northern end of the range? Here is a confusing land of rough heather, rocky canyons and vague paths, where few people tread. Moel Ysgyfarnogod was the only mountain in the area, but a detailed survey of Foel Penolau in 2018 revealed that it also meets the criteria to be a Hewitt. These summits can be combined with a few other tops and a little scrambling for an enjoyable day.

Meaning: Gyrafolen is probably a misspelling or colloquial variation for rowan, "bare hill of the hares".

Summary: A rough walk across several small summits with short sections of scrambling.

Conditions: The terrain is complex, so a day with good visibility is best.

Height Gain: N/A

Approach: The day is started on the west bank of Llyn Trawsfynydd (there is parking near Cae Adda Chapel SH 692352; the base for South Snowdonia Search and Rescue). Walk up the minor road to where a footpath heads west (SH 684358) and take this. At a convenient place bash through heather and climb a stone wall to gain the north-east slopes of Moel y Gyrafolen. A few ruined dwellings can be found up here, curiously absent from the OS map. A faint path occasionally appears, but the direction is obvious: keep heading up to reach the 535m summit.

Ascent: From Moel y Gyrafolen the terrain is complex, and provides a good navigational test when mist descends. The next target is Diffwys to the west. This involves first descending into a small canyon, and then into a much larger one, where a small amount of optional scrambling can be had. Beyond these the flat slabs of Diffwys arrive, with a small path leading the way to the summit (577m).

Move south-west and scramble up to the first summit of Foel Penolau, and then onto the second summit (614m) which consists entirely of rock. A descent can then be made down the far side, where a little rake leads down through the rocky battlements. Unfortunately from here the terrain changes, and an easy walk brings the summit of Moel Ysgyfarnogod (623m).

Usual descents: The best descent, in keeping with the challenges of the day, is to head directly east across pathless ground to reach a track that leads to the roadhead at Cefn Clawdd farm. Road walking then leads back to the start.

Combinations: This entire area is a joy to explore. Perhaps head south towards the summit of Clip, seeking out more micro-scrambles along the way.

Hannah Coustick and Chris Earing appraising the rocky battlements of Foel Penolau on a rather grim day

55. Afon Mawddach (1 or 2 or 3**)

The Afon Mawddach is a Big River. Deep, still pools sleep blackly under a canopy of towering fir trees, and the river is punctuated by rapids and cascades. Escape for the first 0.5 km is difficult due to the steep banks and gorge-side vegetation. This is not a river to be trifled with, and in spate it should be left well alone. Even under normal water levels problems are found; save this one for a prolonged dry spell (these are the conditions that the route description relates to). The scramble described is a traverse with no real vertical height, and begins just north of Ganllwyd where the Mawddach and Eden converge. It features interesting traversing interspersed with walking, and ends at the famous Rhaeadr Mawddach, an ascent of which makes a fine finale to the route.

Meaning: Little Mawdd.

Summary: A scenic traverse along a large river gorge.

Conditions: The route should be tackled in low flow (drought conditions). This is mainly for safety, but also means that clean, water-worn rock is available for scrambling.

Height Gain: 90m (2.5km traverse)

Approach: There is a Forestry Commission car park (SH 732250) on the minor road that heads east at the north end of Ganllwyd. From here walk back along the road towards Glan Eden. Just before the bridge a small path heads left and leads down to the confluence of the Mawddach and Eden.

Ascent: Scramble along the left bank under a pretty wooden bridge (not open to the public; it carries a gas pipe, and is strangely absent from OS maps) to where the river flows down a long straight, flat section. For a traverse to be successful, you should be able to walk along this section whilst keeping reasonably dry feet. As the gorge becomes more imposing clamber along the left bank besides extremely deep water.

Beyond this the atmosphere eases a

little, and a line can be made to suit the scrambler. For a while, the left bank is harder, and the right easier. When a footbridge ahead comes into view, it is best to switch to the left bank. The footbridge offers the first convenient escape, and generally escape is easier for the next 2km of the traverse.

The next section is easy angled and relaxing. The right side of the river can be followed by walking and boulder hopping, or traverses can be contrived on its left side. At one point two channels run around a small central island. Eventually, a more formidable gorge section is reached. Traverse this on the left side and a bridge comes into view as the river turns to the right. Keep on the left and traverse another wall that has a short but tricky down scramble, and a small waterfall appears. One option appears to be to stick to the left bank, and climb up and over the 'boulder' to the left of the waterfall, first by wet ledges. Descend its far side on mossy rock to be confronted by a very deep pool. It might be possible to traverse this wall (probably grade 3) but it is

1. & 2. High water conditions; 3. Shows the same location as 1, but under low flow. This is the 'formidable gorge' section.

unknown if further progress is possible. Instead, quit the gorge below the 'boulder'; rocks in the channel allow the right bank to be gained, followed by a scramble up out of the gorge to the bridge.

After this is a long section of walking. A long shallow pool formed by a small weir is passed, which has a line above it at the far end, presumably to move things across the river. There are more easy traverses, and after passing a mine adit in the right bank some cottages are reached. After these the right bank provides some pleasant traversing before the river bends left by a ruined building. There is then another short walking section. More traversing then leads to the confluence of the Afon Mawddach and the Afon Gain.

Follow the Mawddach (the right hand fork), keeping to its right side. Assorted mine debris litters the area, and the impressive Rhaeadr Mawddach lurks ahead. After traversing some ledges, make a jump/stride across to the left and approach the waterfall. An ascent of this

1. & 2. Scrambling besides deep water; 3. Owain Rice forming the view that discretion is the better part of valour, and opting not to climb a rather full Rhaeadr Mawddach.

1. The view from the first footbridge;
2. Low water levels reveal clean rock;
3. The ascent of Rhaeadr Mawddach.

on its left side is grade 2 and should only be attempted with dry rock. Once started, it is difficult to reverse. Climb the first step to find a surprise: a huge man-eating pothole is hidden on the first ledge! Scary. Don't slip. Walk around the pothole to climb the upper steps. The exact line taken is open to variation, but one option is to climb straight up before then moving right to finish up the 'ridge' next to the falls.

For those with an insatiable gorge appetite turn left and walk down through the relics of the old mines. A small path leads back down to the confluence of the two rivers and the Afon Gain can be followed a short way. This features more interesting traversing, swapping sides where necessary, until a bridge appears. The only continuation is a swim, so leave the gorge and climb up to the bridge. A small path on the right then leads to the impressive Pistyll Cain and its rocky amphitheatre. There is no obvious escape from here, so retrace the route back to the bridge.

Usual Descents: A track on the east side of the river leads back to the car park.

Combinations: The rest of the day is best spent exploring the delights of the Coed y Brenin.

56. Rhobell Fawr East Face (1)

The word 'face' conjures up images of all sorts of vertical excitement, but alas 'east slope' might be a better description. Rhobell Fawr rises above the wooded vales of the Coed y Brenin as a calm and commanding presence. It is an obvious peak, and yet few people stray to visit its summit. Its east side is strewn with small craglets offering a pleasing route to the top, and when combined with nearby Dduallt it makes an excellent mountain day.

Meaning: Big saddle.

Summary: Optional scrambling up rock outcrops.

Conditions: The rock is excellent quality and provides good grip.

Height Gain: 220m

Approach: The quickest approach is from the south, using minor roads (off the A494) then walking along forest roads to Ty-newydd-y-mynydd where an old cottage used to stand (SH 799257). For a mountain day park at the road head in the beautiful Cwm yr Allt Lwyd (SH 787292) and first climb Dduallt by its north ridge. From here head down to the forest (faint paths beside its boundary fence) until you reach an overgrown fire break at approximately SH 804256. Bash west through along this (moss, dead wood, and the occasional spiky fir tree) to reach Ty-newydd-y-mynydd.

Ascent: No real detail is necessary. Head up the slopes picking out the best rock, though climbers might like to take a look at the crag of Graig Fach first. Higher up the best scrambling is found to the right of the dry stone wall that snakes up towards the top. There is a variety of craglets to climb of varying difficulties, but the rock is rough and the scrambling enjoyable. There is a trig point on the summit.

Rhobell Fawr in the rain; pick 'n' mix scrambling over craglets

Usual Descents: To finish the mountain day head north back to Cwm yr Allt Lwyd. Unfortunately, in the lower reaches this involves pathless floundering through heather and bog. To return to the south, drop off the summit over Moel Cors y Garnedd (SH 777236) before making a way back to the car.

Combinations: The best combination is the previously mentioned round of Dduallt and Rhobell Fawr from Cwm yr Allt-lwyd. Rhobell Ganol and Rhobell y Big can also be traversed on the descent.

The Rhinogau and Arenig – Further Scrambling Opportunities

Starting where we finished, in Cwm yr Allt Lwyd is the small gorge and waterfall of Pistyll Dol-cyn-afon (SH 792288). The waterfall itself is probably too steep to ascend, but the gorge above may provide a short trip. It may also be possible to contrive some scrambling on the nearby east face of Dduallt (SH 812273). This is steep and chossy ground, but still looks to hold some esoteric delights.

There is some rock on Arenig Fawr, particularly around its namesake lake, but it is all probably too steep or too broken for the scrambler. Elsewhere in the range, there is a good looking waterfall on the Afon Lliw (SH 823325) near Buarthmeini that would probably go, but would be too brief to be worth seeking out in its own right. Adjacent to this is a small gorge and fall on the Afon Erwent (SH 822329). Further south along this side of the Arenig there are fragments of rocky ground and some interesting terrain; the ravine of the Afon Eiddon (SH 808241) below Craig y Benglog looks very dramatic, but seems unlikely to yield any scrambling.

The Afon Gamlan (SH 722244) in the Coed-y-Brenin has an impressive series of cascades and waterfalls, including the atmospheric Rhaeadr Du. However, the site is exceedingly sensitive, with highly vulnerable populations of SAC-defining oceanic mosses and liverworts on boulder tops. There is a very high risk of damage here and the site should definitely be excluded from scrambling.

In comparison, there is probably endless more scrambling to be had in the Rhinogau. Much of the rock will be best left undocumented; small buttresses, micro-crags, clambering and scrambling in an exploratory fashion. A few can be mentioned here. The south ridge of Rhinog Fach (SH 664269) is a climb graded severe. However, I have frequently looked up from below and wondered whether a hard scrambling ascent might be possible by diversions from the crest. In the other direction the main Rhinogau ridge climbs up to Y Llethr. The path heads off right here, but there is some rock that can be sought out. There is a grade 3 scramble documented on Rhinog Fawr's sprawling south face in "Scrambles and Easy Climbs in Snowdonia". This starts from Bwlch Drws-Ardudwy (approximately SH 663281) and weaves through three tiers of crags. Next comes a long section of walking before more scrambling is contrived around a gully running up towards the summit. The given grade is 3, but I thought only one move deserved this. It could be done at a lower grade by avoiding difficulties. In this sort of complex, broken rocky country specific descriptions are perhaps not helpful. One of the steeper crags in the range is Craig Bodlyn, above its namesake lake (SH 648240). There may well be scrambling here.

Returning to pursuits of a watery nature, the waterfalls on the Afon Cwm Nantcol (SH 607269 and onwards) look entertaining, although they are popular with tourists. Boulders in the river hold many uncommon mosses, such as water grimmia (*Schistidium agassizii*), and the sides of ravine sections are rich in oceanic liverworts.

In the south of the range, the lower section of the Afon Cwm Mynach (SH 688194) might have some gorge characteristics. There is a right of way next to the river, but no access land. Just west of this is the Afon Cwm Llechen (SH 669187) at Bontddu. Again, there are footpaths but no access land, but the gorge does get used by commercial operators. I believe there is an overhanging waterfall and the usual practice is to descend the gorge. However, sensitive species such as deceptive featherwort are present in the gorge, so visits are perhaps best discouraged. The Rhinogau cover a lot of land, and it seems likely that there are a lot streams waiting to be found that will prove to be excellent scrambles.

Cadair Idris

Cadair Idris is undoubtedly the most popular mountain of Southern Snowdonia. People flock here to walk the Minffordd Path, the Pony Path, and the Fox's Path. Climbers visit to tackle the arresting line of the Cyfrwy Arête, or occasionally stray to sample the vegetated cliffs of Craig Cau and the intimidating Pencoed Pillar. In winter, beardy mountaineers come seeking solitude when the snow and ice transforms the ridges and cwms into a glistening and deathly cold cathedral.

Cadair is indeed a fine mountain, or rather, range of mountains. There are seven Hewitts that make up the range, of which Pen y Gadair is the highest (893m). Despite its popularity, it isn't the highest summit in the vicinity (although many people believe it to be). That accolade goes to nearby Aran Fawddwy (905m). Nevertheless, Cadair is still a fine objective, with its splendid array of cwms, ridges, summits and cliffs.

Dolgellau is a decent sized town that makes a convenient base. Kings Youth Hostel is situated several miles west of the town. Corris also makes a useful base, with its independent hostel, bunkhouse and two pubs. The T2 bus runs from Dolgellau to Corris via Minffordd on the A487, and provides access to the east and northern side of Cadair Idris. The T3 runs from Dolgellau to Abermaw (Barmouth), from where the footbridge across the estuary gives a way to explore the western summits of Cadair.

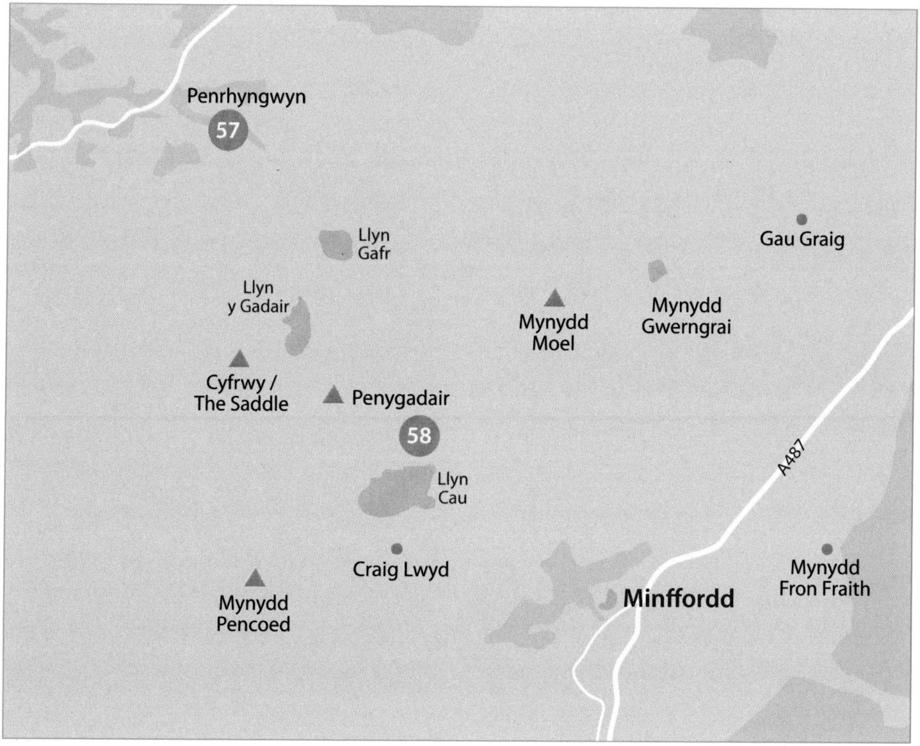
Penrhyngwyn
57
Llyn Gafr
Gau Graig
Llyn y Gadair
Mynydd Moel
Mynydd Gwerngrai
Cyfrwy / The Saddle
Penygadair
58
A487
Llyn Cau
Craig Lwyd
Mynydd Fron Fraith
Mynydd Pencoed
Minffordd

57. Penrhyn-Gwyn Stream (1)

This stream flows down near Ty-nant and the famed Pony Path of Cadair Idris, though is well hidden from prying eyes, as it is hidden by woods and lies in a gorge. It is used by local outdoor centres, so a bypass path appears at points. It is easy to access and therefore is a good choice when pressed for time, or equally good as a scramble to begin a long day on the tops of Cadair. The stream is not named on OS maps.

Meaning: White promontory.

Summary: Generally easy and escapable scrambling in a gorge. There are several waterfalls that cannot be climbed.

Conditions: Much of the rock is very slippery, and socks over boots would be an asset.

Height Gain: 150m

Approach: There is parking at the base of the Pony Path (SH 698153). Cross the road and walk up the Pony Path beside a stream. After a short distance the Pony Path turns right over a footbridge; the track that continues straight on leads in the desired direction but there is no legal access here. It is better to follow the Pony Path for another 190 m to where it reaches access land. From here turn left and follow the access land to rejoin the earlier continuation track. Pass through a gate and follow the track left. Beyond some slate gateposts (but no gate) the quarry of Penrhyn-Gwyn is reached. Pass the first ruined building below a long incline, and look left where a muddy path leads down into the gorge to the stream at SH 701150.

Ascent: Boulder hop up the gorge, until the first step is reached. This, and the next one, can both be taken easily on the left to arrive at a waterfall that cascades out of a chute. Avoid this by leaving the gorge on the left where a path climbs out. Up here is an old pipe, and the stream can be regained. The next step is small, but not as easy as it looks; climb it on the right, in the water, and continue past some thin pipes and (on the right) stone walls to reach a fork in the gorge. There is a mine adit on the right here. Walk up the left fork first to find a pool and a waterfall, with no obvious continuation. Retreat and try the right fork, which ends with an identical result. Retreat again, and escape up the bilberry-studded ground between the two branches. This is quite airy and there are views of a dank amphitheatre and a large waterfall in the left gorge, and another large waterfall in the right.

Above the waterfall the left branch can be accessed again (the right branch has several impossible falls and is best avoided), though now the stream is much less gorge-like. At first it consists of boulders and the occasional traverse, but further on easy-angled but slippery waterslides dominate. Progress is barred at a pool and waterfall. Escape the gorge, and this is where the scramble ends.

Usual Descents: The Fox's Path is nearby, and can be followed down to Llyn Gwernan. From here, a path leads round the east side of the lake to gain a right of way that heads back to the car park. If time is short, the road also offers a way back.

Penrhyn-Gwyn Stream

Combinations: Above the scramble, the northern ramparts of Cadair Idris call out to the explorer. The Fox's Path leads through scree to the summit, or a traverse west leads to the Pony Path, and a friendlier ascent. For scramblers, the Cyfrwy Arête is nearby, and is an easy climb or hard scramble. Once on the ridge, there are numerous summits to the east and west that can satisfy the need for a long tramp.

58. Tapia Llwydion Slabs (1/2**)

Cwm Cau is the jewel in Cadair's crown. Its blue lake sits hemmed in by a giant cirque of rocks, with the vegetated and brooding precipice of Craig Cau stealing the show. The crag is a towering mass of steep, blank walls, grassy ledges, and deep gullies. From across the lake the relief of the cliff is not obvious, but when descending the Stone Shoot (the scree rake at the north end of the cliffs) the crag takes on a more three-dimensional appearance, and the vertiginous obelisk of Pencoed Pillar finally reveals itself. This is not a cliff for the inexperienced mountaineer. However, on tearing one's gaze away to the north wall of the cwm a gentler sight is seen. Above the lake a series of slabs and heathery slopes rise up to the summit ridge of Pen y Gadair. A diff climb (combined with a grade 3 scramble) was described here in "Scrambles and Easy Climbs in Snowdonia" but the terrain is just as (perhaps more) amenable to low-grade scrambling. The crag is not named on OS maps, and I have therefore taken the name from the aforementioned guidebook.

Meaning: Grey crags.

Summary: The lower section climbs the main sweep of slabs, broken up by heathery ledges. Higher up the scrambling is less continuous and the best line must be sought.

Conditions: The rock itself is clean and offers excellent grip but the route is probably worth avoiding in the wet.

Height Gain: 230m

Approach: From the car park (SH 732115) take the Minffordd Path to Llyn Cau. From here the slabs are clearly visible to the right and above the lake. Follow the path around the north side of the lake then break up towards the slabs, aiming for the far left end where a gully bounds the edge of the slabs (SH 716126).

Ascent: Climb up the slabs at will, seeking the best and most continuous sections of rock. The rock is extremely grippy but lacks the positive handholds some will be accustomed too. Heathery runnels can be used for easier progress. On the heathery terraces that break up the route traces of a path can be followed, suggesting that this route is known to other scramblers. Towards the top of the slabs the rock narrows and a nose of rock marks the 'summit' of this section, with a miniature col behind it. The best is unfortunately now over. Continuing straight up by walking and scrappy scrambling will bring the summit ridge. Moving right will give access to harder and slightly more sustained scrambling. Either way, an in-depth route description would be superfluous. From the summit ridge the trig point of Pen y Gadair is a 0.5km walk away to the left.

Usual Descents: From the summit head off down the Minffordd Path. In mist this can take some finding, and it is possible to become drawn west down the Pony Path by mistake. From the low point between Pen y Gadair and Craig Cau the Stone Shoot leads down to Cwm Cau. This is loose, steep, and direct.

The Tapia Llwydion Slabs offer enjoyable scrambling with excellent views

Combinations: The Minffordd Path can be followed over the summit of Craig Cau (also listed as Mynydd Pencoed and Craig Cwm Amarch). Alternatively, head east from Pen y Gadair to the summit of Mynydd Moel, and then back down to the slate footbridge over the Nant Cadair.

Cadair Idris – Further Scrambling Opportunities

The Nant Cadair tumbles playfully down besides the steep start of the Minfford Path. Steep sides rise up covered in trees, bracken, brambles and heather, whilst glimpses behind reveal the soft, green fields of the valley. The stream looks inviting, but the vegetation is very sensitive, particularly the ravine sides. As such, gorge scramblers should leave this stream unexplored.

Just north of the western end of the Cadair Idris ridge is Bryn Brith (383m). It is everything a miniature mountain should be and provides fine views in all directions, especially back over the scenic Llynnau Cregennen to Cadair. Its south-west ridge offers a few micro scrambles, and then by proceeding along to Pared y Cefn Hir a few more short walls can be found. Nearby Llyn Pen Moelyn is also worth a short diversion. In the same area is the Afon Arthog (SH 647144) which features numerous small waterfalls. I believe this gets used by outdoor centres as a gorge scramble.

On Cadair Idris itself is the intriguing north ridge of Mynydd Moel (SH 727137). I've come across no mention of it, but peering down from the summit are traces of footfall. Perhaps they were lost souls hoping for a way off the mountain where there is none, or perhaps it offers a scramble/walk/climb to the summit. Who knows? Also on Mynydd Moel is a chossy spur (SH 731136) that stands slightly aside from the main bulk of the hill. It is split by vegetated rakes and gullies, so it may be possible to execute a zig-zagging way up. Rock is plentiful along the rest of the northern scarp of the Cadair Idris massif, so brave explorers may well discover more interesting scrambles. The slopes above Cwm Rhwyddfor on the south-east side of the massif are also garlanded with crags and scree gullies (SH 738127) but it would be a steep slog upwards to find anything of interest.

Bryn Brith

The Rest of Wales

The routes described in this book are merely a small selection, restricted to north Wales. Other possible scrambles in north Wales have been discussed at the end of each chapter, but here I shall briefly note where possibilities might lie in the rest of Wales.

Starting in north-east Wales: not far outside of Wrecsam (Wrexham) at Bwlchgwyn is the Nant y Frith gorge (SJ 265541). The gorge is deep but a footpath leads into it. There is a least one waterfall, but as the gorge is about 2.5 km long an investigation may be worthwhile. Above Llangollen is Creigiau Eglwyseg (SJ 221445). Most of the rock here is steep, but some clambering might be found in the gullies on the east of the escarpment, and a day walking this area would still be a day well spent. Just south of Llangollen is a quiet little valley of pasture and forest, where the adjacent streams of the Nant y Bache (SJ 202404) and Cyflymen (SJ 205399) are found. There are some waterfalls marked on the map, and both run in likely-looking valleys, although the land here is not access land. At the east end of the Vale of Llangollen is the Nant y Belan gorge (SJ 303414). This is a deep, wooded gorge near Wynnstay Park with no public access, but it appears impressive on the map. At the west end of the Vale of Llangollen, above Corwen, the Nant Cawrddu flows briefly down a short rocky gorge (according to the map at SJ 079428). Footpaths in the vicinity would allow a closer look. A few miles south from Corwen is the village of Cynwyd. The Afon Trystion is used by commercial groups in descent, starting from the reservoir at SJ 066405. An ascent might be feasible, but there is no access land. Eastwards over the mountain is the remote Afon Ceiriog gorge which looks promising (SJ 130366).

Moving south into the Hirnant hills we come to Llyn Efyrnwy (Lake Vrynwy). A close look at waterfalls on the Afon Eiddew (SH 953246) at the north end of the lake would probably prove fruitful, and some of the other streams around the lake have some cascades on (e.g. Hirddu Fawr, SH 955213). Experienced scramblers with a head for heights might try and pick a way up the spiky ribs of Craig yr Ogof (SH 914246).

Onwards into the nearby Aran hills. The ridge of Tap Nyth yr Eryr (SH 905217) attracts the eye and can be scrambled. The Afon Dyfi below it (SH 896216) has numerous small waterfalls and looks worthwhile, and its tributary, the Nant Llewelyn Goch (SH 901215), also has some falls. This entire area is crammed with streams and crags that clamour for attention; the Nant y Gwnfa (SH 915219) is a steep, mountainous cleft, probably out of bounds for mere scramblers. The same is probably true of the Nant Lledfron (SH 895201) and its shattered ravine. Most of the neighbouring cwms have streams, but Llam Lloi, where a stream runs in a narrow ravine, (SH 918183) might be the best to investigate closer. In nearby Cwm Cywarch there are more streams, of which Camddwr (SH 850199) looks the most promising.

The Nant Helygog technically belongs to the Aran hills. Lying in the woods near the village of Brithdir is a spectacular and deep gorge – there's no scramble here, but gorge-lovers will appreciate the spectacle nonetheless. The gorge is reached from the bridge at SH 788197 – this first section is not access land, although there is access land a few hundred metres further down through the woods. Curiously, there are also some wooden posts about, perhaps the remains of an old waymarked trail? The gorge itself can be viewed from the west bank, and is a stupendous sight – a deep, incised ravine cloaked in deciduous trees, with numerous waterfalls thundering below. A word of caution – the edge of the gorge is quite vegetated, and in places it is difficult to judge what is safe to stand on and what is just plantlife. The falls are mentioned in the "Cambrian Travellers Guide in Every Direction" (1840) which notes they have been "hitherto unnoticed by any tourist" and suggest the largest fall is 16.5 m. The nearby gorge of the Afon Celynog might be more feasible as a scramble, but some waterfalls might be insurmountable. Nevertheless, there is a pleasant path along its east bank starting from Pont y Sel at SH 795204. This is a delightful area for wandering the paths and lanes, and a foray can be made onto the Aran hills if more mountainous terrain is desired.

There are a few possible leads in the Tarren hills. Just along the road from Abergynolwyn is the Nant Iago (SH 695072) where some waterfalls are shown on the map. However, access land doesn't extend to the road, so an approach would be convoluted. On the same side of the Tarren hills, there are numerous waterfalls on the Nant Dolgoch (SH 653042).

Heading on, we pass south of Machynlleth. Here the peaks are less pronounced than further north, but the high ground is extensive and wild and unfrequented. A diversion off the mountain road between Machynlleth and Dylife leads into Cwm Hengwm. Thick plantation cloaks the cwm, but the map shows waterfalls on the Afon Hengwm (SN 774932) and a gorge on the Nant Tarren Fedw Ddu (SN 783935). The map also marks tiny Llyn y Delyn (SN 772936) which is apparently a kettle hole, though I have not visited it. Just east of Cwm Hengwm is Tarren Bwlch Gwyn which has three streams: Rhaeadr Ddu (SN 811933) which is probably a chossy gully climb not a scramble; Rhaeadr Wen (SN 815932) which looks to give some scrambling in a shallow gorge; and a stream unnamed on maps (SN 816935) that also runs in a shallow gorge. North-east from here is a huge shattered chasm (SN 827949) where the Afon Dulas drains Glaslyn. I've no idea if an ascent is within the realms of possibility, but no doubt an attempt would be a real adventure. Just across the mountain road, two other smaller ravines are found adjacent at SN 841965 (on access land) and SN 845965 (not on access land). Finally, at Dylife is the impressive waterfall Ffrwd Fawr (SN 872939) which is obviously too steep for scrambling. Some scrambling might be found lower down below the waterfall, but the neighbouring Nant Ddeiliog (SN 868952) has a gentler gradient and might be worth a look.

A modicum of rocky scrambling could probably be had on Craig y March (SN 806881) on Pumlumon, but only if passing (it's a long walk in). On the 'popular' side of Pumlumon, near Eisteddfa Gurig, is the Afon Tarennig (SN 794841). This runs over rock steps in a miniature ravine and would probably make a good diversion whilst heading to Pen Pumlumon Fawr. 6km south is the magnificent gorge of the Nant

Rhuddnant (SN 796783). The steep slopes of conifers and heather are over 100 m high. The river occasionally gets descended by kayakers, but I am unsure whether an ascent is possible; it would probably result in a very memorable day. In the next cwm north is the Afon Myherin (SN 798806) – brave scramblers might be able to tackle the tallest waterfall head on, or it may prove to be too difficult. In the vicinity of Devil's Bridge there are several deep gorges, but expeditions into these probably entail canyoning, rather than scrambling tactics. Near Rhaeadr, the Nant Gwynllyn (SN 941694) tumbles over several small falls and looks escapable. The Rhiwnant (SN 884608) above the Caban-coch reservoir is a quiet valley that leads up to Drygarn Fawr. There are a few waterfalls, but nothing worth seeking out. Its tributary, the Nant y Carw (SN 876605), looks more promising. Nonetheless, this is fine walking country, and well worth exploring.

Geographically, this is where my suggestions end. The remainder of mid Wales will almost certainly have some gorge scrambles waiting to be found. In south Wales there are plenty of big gorges and famous waterfalls, and some commercial companies do operate. Although I am not 100% sure, I suspect they mostly descend the gorges in a canyoning fashion.

Nant y Gwnfa

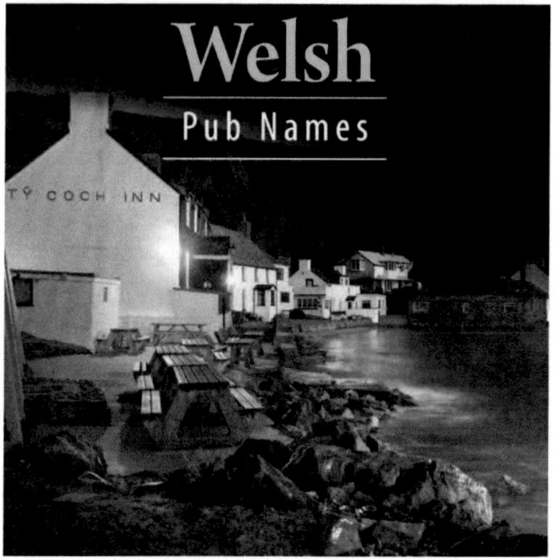
Welsh
Pub Names
TŶ COCH INN

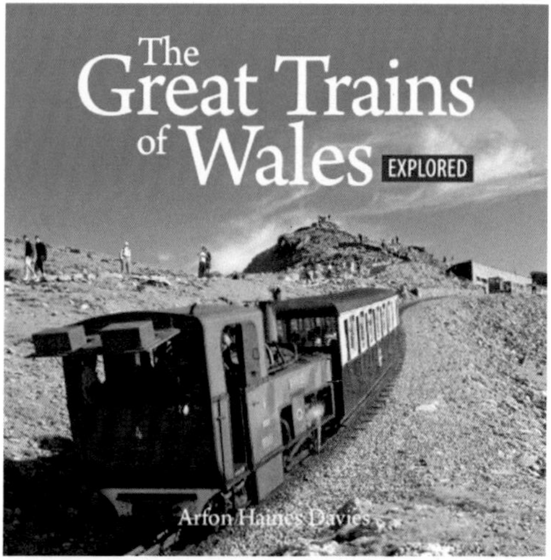
The
Great Trains
of Wales
EXPLORED
Arfon Haines Davies

Snowdon
and its
Villages
EXPLORED

Battles FOR Wales
1136
Myrddin ap Dafydd

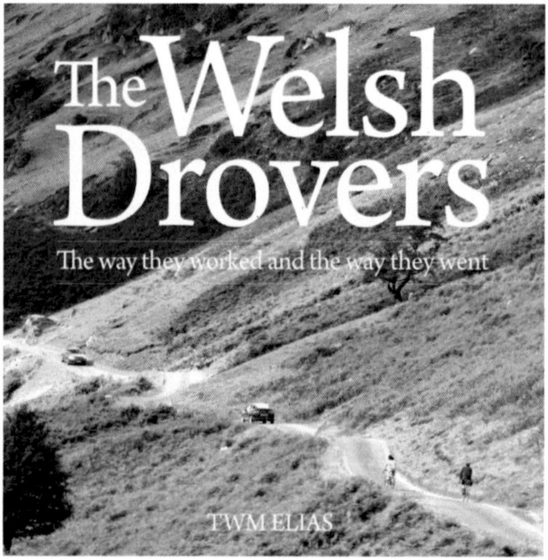
The Welsh Drovers
The way they worked and the way they went
TWM ELIAS

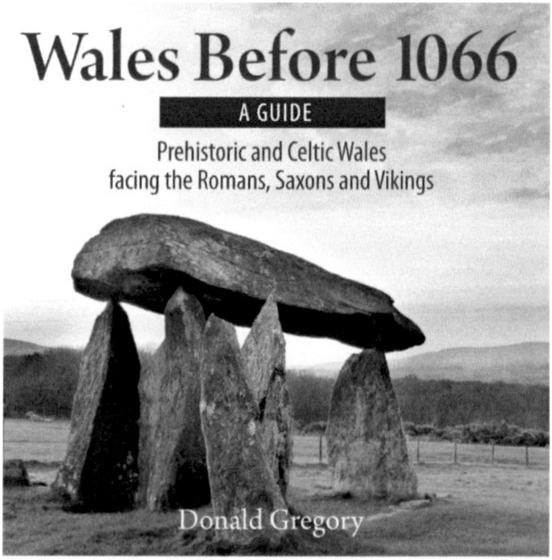
Wales Before 1066
A GUIDE
Prehistoric and Celtic Wales
facing the Romans, Saxons and Vikings
Donald Gregory

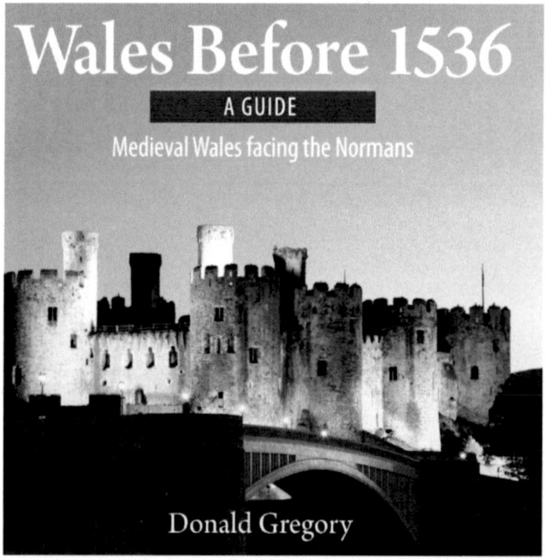
Wales Before 1536
A GUIDE
Medieval Wales facing the Normans
Donald Gregory

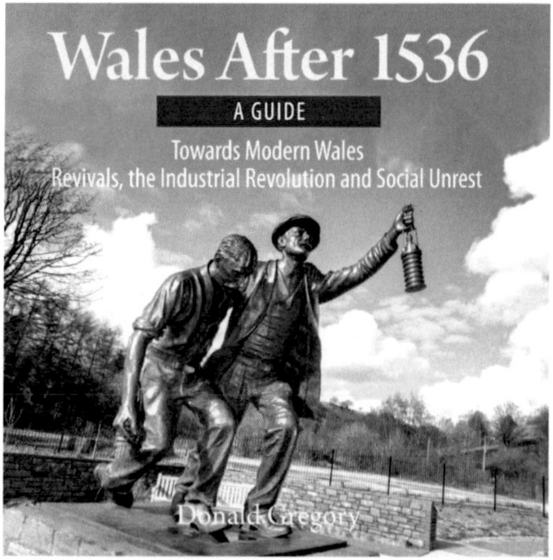
Wales After 1536
A GUIDE
Towards Modern Wales
Revivals, the Industrial Revolution and Social Unrest
Donald Gregory